Enterprise Risk Management
STRAIGHT TO THE VALUE
How to Uncover the Value of ERM

Al Decker
Donna Galer

Table of Contents

Chapter 5 49

The Value of Applying ERM to Corporate Strategy

Chapter 6 67

The Value of Applying ERM to Mergers and Acquisitions

Chapter 15 ....**183**

Final Thoughts

Preface

Boards of directors, chief executive officers, and other senior executives already know that all actions come with risk. They would not be in high-level positions if they were not men and women- of action who were able to deal successfully with risk. Thus, the notion that a formal business process for identifying and managing risks is necessary has taken a long time to penetrate the collective corporate mindset. Now, all but a few would deny that this dynamic and disruptive marketplace demands a robust and holistic approach to managing risk.

The purpose of this book is to provide a clear and broad analysis of the value that an enterprise risk management (ERM) approach creates. Common business actions that generate substantial uncertainty and have great potential to cause significant gain or loss will be reviewed in the context of how ERM, if applied, could manage the risk to the advantage the organization.

The words uncertainty and risk will often be used interchangeably in this book. This is a practice that has been adopted by most academics, practitioners, and consultants as well as trade associations.

The value of ERM is described for each of the following business areas:

- Corporate strategy
- Mergers and acquisitions
- New marketing ventures
- Talent management/human resources
- Change management
- Finance and financial risk
- The supply chain and sourcing
- Governance

There are indeed quantitative and qualitative benefits from ERM. This book will attempt to show how to recognize and/or measure both. As most readers know, it is difficult to numerically capture a financial debacle that did not happen or a reputational snafu that did not take place. It is also hard to quantify how much profit comes from getting the management team aligned to the corporate strategy, but few argue against the necessity of achieving alignment in order to achieve strategy and profitability goals. These measurement difficulties do not make the benefit of dealing with risk or creating alignment any less real or important.

Nevertheless, there are many quantitative benefits that could be derived from a robust ERM implementation, such as lower stock price volatility, better credit ratings, lower cost of capital, less litigation expense, lower claims cost, and lower insurance costs. Softer benefits include fewer surprises and less drain on management time; enhanced reputation; more lead time to mitigate risks that cannot be eliminated, avoided, or transferred; and better preparedness when risk materializes.

No process or its implementation is perfect. That does not negate the value that can be derived from a continuously improving application of a good process. We strongly believe ERM will create value for any size of organization and that it is well worth the effort.

Chapter 1

Definition of ERM: A Strategic Approach

The logical place to begin a discussion of the value of a business approach or process is with a definition and description. This chapter draws heavily from our first book, ***Enterprise Risk Management: Straight to the Point***.

Enterprise risk management (ERM) involves viewing risk holistically and horizontally across an organization. Both insurable and non-insurable risks are identified across all facets and disciplines of an entity, with the objective being to eliminate, ameliorate, or transfer such risks—or to be prepared to accept them.

ERM is a process. Its goal is to focus on and address risks that threaten achievement of the organization's strategy and long-term goals. The starting point for implementing the process is, in fact, the organization's strategy.

Most organizations big and small have a strategic plan. If not, they at least have long-range objectives and goals. In either case, there is a vision of the future wherein certain results will have been accomplished in order to ensure the success and profitability of the organization. Anything that might stand in the way of successful execution of the strategy and accomplishment of goals has to be identified and addressed in order to maximize the chance of success.

The ERM process starts with an explicit statement or understanding of the corporate strategy, goals, and objectives as well as the underlying goals and objectives of each functional area. The next step is to identify the major risks associated with these goals and objectives. Then, risks are quantified and qualified in terms of their likelihood and impact, then prioritized and paired with mitigation plans.

There are two widely recognized frameworks for embedding ERM into an organization: COSO (Committee of Sponsoring Organizations) Enterprise Risk Management—Integrated Framework, and ISO (International Organization for Standardization) standard 31000: Risk Management—Principles and Guidelines. There are some differences between these frameworks, and each has its share of proponents. Regardless of their differences, both provide meaningful context for ERM within the organization. The ERM process steps discussed in this book can work within both of these frameworks.

Following is an overall view of the process that will be referred to in this book.

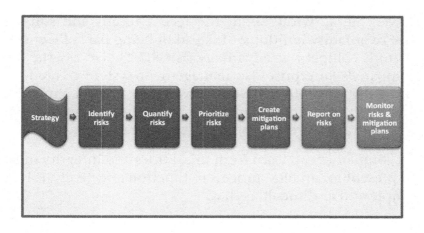

What ERM Is, and What It Is Not

A word about what ERM is not. It is different than older forms of risk management that focused on insurable risks, safety, and claims handling. It is more strategic and encompassing in terms of the risks it seeks to identify and deal with. In addition, it involves the entire organization by creating a risk-aware culture. ERM is not compliance, nor is it an audit function. However, both of these functions have some role to play in risk identification and mitigation. In addition, ERM is not a substitute for strategic planning, although there is a nexus between them. Chapter 5 will spell this out clearly.

Beyond the Process

The process is important, but implementing a process is a Pyrrhic victory within a culture that lacks ethics or integrity. ERM requires transparency, honesty, insightfulness, and long-term perspective. If managers do not expose or act upon risks because they worry this will affect their near-term incentives, or if employees do not care about others or the future well being of the company, or if the C-suite is unwilling to champion the process consistently, then the process will not provide the value it is capable of.

Steven Slezak wrote about the recent recalls and suits at GM over faulty ignitions: "Instead of being part of General Motors' competitive advantage, as CRO Thelen asserts, the company's enterprise risk management system created for GM a distinct competitive disadvantage. When companies mistake process for execution, 'terrible things' can happen. CEO Barra is correct, this should surprise no one."[1]

All companies can learn from this. Ethics and integrity must be present for an ERM process to function effectively. It is as simple and as difficult as that.

Chapter 2

Comparison of ERM vs. RM

There is a substantive difference between older or less encompassing forms of risk management (RM) and enterprise risk management.

ERM	RM
Addresses both non-insurable and insurable risks	Addresses primarily insurable risks
Focuses first on the strategic risks and how to manage them	Lacks major focus on strategic risks
Is a continuous loop process	Is most concerned with annual insurance program renewals
Is internally and externally focused	Is more internally focused
Involves multifunctional leadership through an ERM committee, for example	Lacks multifunctional leadership, more siloed
Promotes an open dialogue and risk awareness	Does little to promote open dialogue and risk awareness

As with most comparisons, the difference between ERM and RM in any single organization may not be as stark as the chart depicts. Or it may be even sharper. Many organizations are still transitioning to ERM and may be someplace in the middle in terms of their evolution.

What Spurred the Evolution?

There was a time when a fire could wipe out a business. Those were the days when many companies operated out of one or only a handful of locations and were laden with inventory. Firefighting was less sophisticated and fire stations were few and far between. Insurance was not always purchased. Physical property risk was a major concern. Buying property insurance against fire loss was a big deal in many ways. It was a way to protect the company from total destruction and closure, and it was a significant expense. Today, warehousing and manufacturing are more distributed and protected, just-in-time inventory control is commonplace, firefighting is light years ahead of where it was at the beginning of the last century, and it is a given that companies will have property insurance. Companies have other risk priorities because property damage by fire (although it can still occur) is nonetheless generally well managed.

Over the last few decades, there has been an even greater transformation of what kinds of risks companies are most concerned about. This does not mean that older types of risks do not need to be managed. They do, and most are. Rather, it means that old categories of risk are routinely handled, and new categories of risk have emerged and are still emerging that require innovative thinking to be managed.

Compared to the past, more companies risk failure due to technological obsolescence rather than physical loss, face large liability losses due to financial dealings rather than bodily injury or physical damage to another's property, risk business interruption due to a storm thousands of miles away from the point of sale rather than a local storm, and risk losing customers over social media hullabaloos rather than a gradual product life cycle disenchantment. These few examples signify a sea change in the world of business and show why a change in the mindset, processes, and practices of risk management is so necessary. Hence, the shift from a less strategic focus to a more strategic focus and from a silo-like approach to a multifunctional approach in the way that risk is managed has taken place. Another shift is from insurance being the primary solution for mitigating risk to other solutions or a greater mix of solutions.

Strategic risk grows	• Technological obsolesence—e.g., Internet disintermediation for distributors or middlemen, such as bookstores, travel agents, etc.
Litigation risks grow/ shareholder suits	• Botched M&As • IPO abuses • Financial reporting debacles
Supply chain risks grow	• Greater geographic spread into higher risk areas for procurement (political, natural catastrophes, other risks)

What Skills Does the ERM Leader Need Now?

The chief risk officer (CRO) or ERM leader needs first and foremost to be a businessperson. The individual needs to have a well-rounded understanding of how a business runs and preferably how a business in a particular industry runs. Some of the skills and knowledge required are:

- Ability to think strategically
- Ability to communicate clearly
- Ability to interpret data
- Ability to link cause and effect
- Ability to see trends
- Ability to problem solve
- Ability to innovate
- Ability to build teams
- Ability to gain consensus
- Ability to manage others
- Ability to manage projects
- Working knowledge of ERM principles
- Working knowledge of insurance principles
- Working knowledge of basic business finance
- Working knowledge of strategic planning principles
- Working knowledge of business operations in the various business functions
- Working knowledge of governance principles
- Working knowledge of social media
- Working knowledge of software used for communicating and reporting
- Working knowledge of project management techniques
- Working knowledge of primary and secondary research techniques

- Working knowledge of current events and business issues

- Working knowledge of the particular industry

This list is not exhaustive. It should demonstrate that the incumbent to a CRO or ERM leader position must have broad business acumen as opposed to narrow depth in one field. Although the individual may have previously held a more narrow position, the key is whether or not the individual has the requisite skills and knowledge to handle a broader and more integrative role than what they may have had previously.

To do well in the role, the individual must have credibility with the C-suite so that risk gets the attention it needs. Regardless of how that credibility is earned, it will be necessary for building the right culture to focus on managing risk throughout the organization.

In many organizations, the ERM function and the risk management/insurance function are separate. Each can provide independent value, but the greatest value for an organization comes when these functions cooperate and work together.

While ERM focuses on more strategic risks, RM focuses on basic risks that are covered by internal safety measures, insurance, or other transfer mechanisms. RM also manages, with or without third-party assistance, insurance claims, workers compensation cases, claims litigation, etc.

A synergistic benefit can be realized from the work each function performs, and the value of their efforts as a whole become greater than their individual benefits.

Chapter 3

ERM's Broad Benefits: Qualitative Value

Qualitative Value Is Value

In general, the demonstration of value is a fundamental problem for enterprise risk management, which may be one of the factors that inhibit the growth of sound ERM practices within an organization.

Empirical evidence on the value of ERM, especially for large organizations, has been elusive. In a report published by the Society of Actuaries, the authors write, "Despite the substantial interest in ERM by academics and practitioners and the abundance of survey evidence on the prevalence and characteristics of ERM programs . . . , there is an absence of empirical evidence regarding the impact of such programs on firm value. The absence of clear empirical evidence on the value of ERM programs continues to limit the growth of these programs."[1] As a result, "executives are 'justifiably uncomfortable making a deeper commitment to ERM without a clear and quantifiable business case.'"

When things are going well and there are no surprises, it is more difficult determine the value of ERM. Yet, when surprises occur the value of ERM becomes more apparent.

This chapter will assist an organization in determining the value of ERM in advance of risk events occurring.

A Management Practice

ERM, as defined in COSO's Enterprise Risk Management—Integrated Framework, is "a process, effected by an entity's board of directors, management and other personnel, applied in strategy setting and across the enterprise, designed to identify potential events that may affect the entity, to provide reasonable assurance regarding the achievement of entity objectives."

By this definition, and in its purest form, ERM is essentially a management practice. One interesting aspect of the majority of management practices or philosophies is that they are not something required by regulators or others. However, they are assessed by rating agencies either implicitly or explicitly. And good managers intuit their value. The best reason to engage in ERM is that it makes justifiably good business sense.

Many popular concepts, such as GRC (governance, risk, and compliance), attempt to align or associate ERM with compliance. Unlike compliance, there are currently no laws and only a circumscribed number of industry regulations that require a company to undertake an ERM initiative. ERM is something a company does to improve itself.

But if law or regulation does not require an ERM program, it must represent value for an organization to voluntarily initiate an ERM program. Perhaps the best way to determine the value of ERM is by contrast and comparison to other well-established and respected management practices. Mathematically speaking, if A = B and B = C, then A = C. So, if ERM can be found to be similar in practice and approach to other value-producing and well-respected management practices, then ERM, properly implemented, can be viewed as also providing value and benefits.

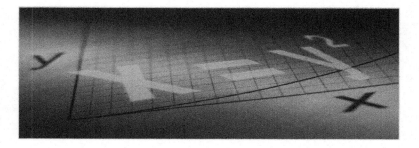

For example, it is clear that management by objectives (MBO) is a well-respected, value-producing management practice that has been implemented in thousands of companies around the world. Its longevity as a management practice alone points to its being viewed as a valuable approach to business management. But to relate the practice specifically to a measured increase in earnings per share, or in other quantifiable terms, is difficult.

As you will see in the following comparisons, much of the value and benefit of formalized management disciplines can be found in the process itself.

Few companies, large or small, can be run without a host of processes, many of which are not measured in quantifiable terms but are considered essential.

Process	Quantified: Yes	Quantified: No
Strategic planning process		X
Budgeting process		X
Performance management process		X
New employee orientation process		X
Legal contract review process		X

ERM as Compared to MBO

MBO may be the most widely accepted management practice today. It concentrates attention on the accomplishment of objectives through participation of all concerned parties. MBO is based on the belief that people perform better when they know what is expected of them and they can relate their personal goals to organizational objectives.

First introduced in 1954 by Peter Drucker, the premise of MBO is that when an organization clearly establishes definable objectives that are developed by and/or have the buy-in of both management and staff, the organization stands a far better chance of actually accomplishing those objectives than if they are simply dictated from the top down. MBO ensures that managers and staff have somewhere to go before they set out on a journey.

While that may seem obvious, Drucker pointed out that managers often lose sight of their objectives because of something he called the "activity trap." They get so involved in their current activities that they forget their original purpose. In some cases, they become engrossed in daily activities as a means of avoiding the uncomfortable truth about their ability to meet objectives.

The same can be said about managing risk. If major risks to an organization's objectives are clearly identified and understood (or bought into) by managers and staff, it is far more likely that those risks will be managed or mitigated, thus helping ensure that objectives are achieved. In addition, just as Drucker said about managers losing sight of their objectives due to becoming engrossed in day-to-day activities, unless properly documented and understood, managers may also lose sight of the risks that may be affecting the outcome of their objectives.

Likewise, senior management may become so involved in managing quarterly results that focusing on longer-term risk seems to be a distraction from achieving analysts' expectations. In other cases they may be trying to avoid the truth about their risk.

MBO was an integral part of the "HP way," the widely acclaimed management style of Hewlett-Packard in its early days as a computer company. At every level within Hewlett-Packard, managers had to develop objectives and integrate them with those of other managers and of the company as a whole. This was done by producing written plans showing what people needed to achieve if they were to reach those objectives. The plans were then shared with others in the corporation and coordinated.

The implementation of an ERM process includes:

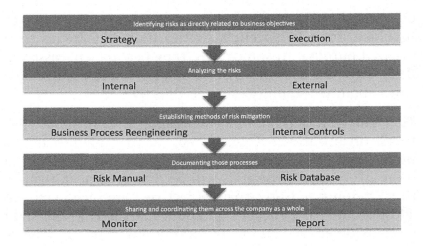

If we overlay the ERM process with the principles of MBO, each of these steps will involve not only the management team but also staff, who are often much closer to the day-to-day risks. The identification process becomes more granular and perhaps more realistic, analyzing the risk becomes more grounded in real-world likelihood and consequence, risk mitigation becomes more practical, and the documented results become more easily shared and understood by operational teams.

The planning process in an MBO-managed organization involves many layers of management and staff. The plan, when it finally emerges, would then have the commitment of all of them.

When the ERM process is developed with the involvement of all levels of personnel across the organization, managers obtain understanding of risks under their responsibility, obtain understanding of how risk is managed in other areas of the business, and gain insight into best practices across the company, and the company develops a well-defined risk culture that can instill great confidence in the company's continued success for shareholders, customers, and employees.

A primary goal of MBO is to direct operational performance toward the achievement of specific objectives and goals. Similarly, a primary goal of ERM is to ensure the achievement of goals and objectives. Both MBO and ERM demand management involvement on an ongoing basis.

Clearly, the desired outcomes of MBO and ERM are nearly identical, and both share many of the same principles. It follows then that the value derived from ERM can be viewed in the same way as it is for MBO.

Much of the value and many of the benefits of formalized management disciplines are found in the process itself. The following are a number of well-identified and clearly understood benefits of MBO.

- Improved planning: Like MBO, ERM involves participative decision making, which makes risk identification explicit and mitigation plans more realistic. It focuses attention on risks that impact key business goals in key result areas. ERM forces managers to think in terms of the impact on objectives of risk rather than simply on the risk. It encourages people to establish specific risk mitigation instead of depending on hunches or guesswork. An integrated hierarchy of risk management is created throughout the organization. Precise mitigation objectives and measures indicating goal accomplishment are laid down.

- Coordination: Whereas MBO helps to clarify the structure and goals of the organization, ERM helps to clarify the structure and goals of the organization in consideration of the risks. Clarifying risk management objectives enables individuals at various levels to have a common understanding of the risk involved. Every individual knows clearly his or her role in the organization and the elements of risk he or she is expected to monitor and manage. Interlinking of corporate, unit, and individual objectives helps in the decentralization of authority and fixation of responsibility. ERM results in a clarification of organizational roles and structure with respect to risk management. It promotes and integrated view of risk and encourages interdepartmental coordination.

- Motivation and commitment: Clearly one of the major benefits and values of MBO is the participation of staff in goal setting. It improves their commitment to performance. In a well-defined ERM program, the participation of staff in risk management decisions will improve their commitment to mitigating those risks. Corporate risk management is translated into personal risk management at all levels and integrated with individual performance. The improved communications across the enterprise that result from the formal implementation of ERM helps ensure that risk is well understood and effectively managed.

- Executive development: MBO is a kind of self-discipline. It stresses a long-term perspective and self-development. MBO releases potential by providing opportunities for learning, innovation, and creativity. It encourages initiative and growth by stretching the capabilities of executives. MBO makes possible a high degree of self-control by individual managers and increases decentralization of authority. Just as MBO is a strategy for developing self-discipline for management in meeting objectives, ERM instills a form of self-discipline in managers who are not adept at identifying and managing risk. As individuals progress through the organizational ranks, they become more capable of identifying and managing risk. In a risk management culture, risk is not feared. Rather, it is understood and managed like any other business issue. MBO and ERM make individuals better managers.

- Organizational change and development: MBO provides a framework for planned changes; ERM provides a framework for the management of risk. It enables managers to identify and manage the unexpected. It helps them identify issues across the organizational structure and processes that are subject to the impact of the unexpected (risk). In this way, ERM improves the capacity of the organization to cope with its changing environment.

It is clear then that the value and each of the most well defined benefits of MBO can also be ascribed to ERM.

The value of ERM can also be seen in the symbiotic relationship it has to MBO. ERM enhances the MBO process in most of its major elements by broadening the view of the objectives and by ensuring consideration of risks that could cause those objectives to fail. Likewise, ERM benefits from the rigors established by a strong company commitment to MBO. Business objectives are broken down into more manageable components that have the buy-in of management as well as staff. This provides for a much higher degree of risk understanding and appreciation at all levels of the organization.

Chapter 4

ERM's Broad Benefits: Quantitative Value

Most executives agree that managing risk on an enterprise-wide basis has value. As discussed in the previous chapter, ERM brings many benefits to an organization. These benefits include such things as:

- Contributing to the successful outcomes of strategic plans

- Improved decision making

- Improved execution of business plans

- Improved planning and coordination between functions

- Clear understanding of risks under a manager's own responsibility

- Insight into best risk management practices across the company

But all of these benefits, while clearly important to any organization, are viewed by many as soft benefits. They are indeed undeniably important, but unfortunately not likely to spur significant interest or resource commitment by senior management. Like any other investment in time or money, unless we can see tangible benefits, unless it is something that can actually be measured and quantified, it won't be taken seriously or perhaps even get done at all.

There is an old adage, what gets measured, gets managed. That certainly implies that it is important to measure the progress and value of an ERM process so that it can be well managed.

The previous chapter discussed the qualitative value of ERM. In this chapter the methods for quantitatively measuring the value of ERM will be explored.

Let's begin by underscoring the fact that there is no magic wand here. There are no quick methods, no easily developed dashboards, and no ways to broadly quantify the value. Implemented properly, ERM should move quickly from a broad, unfocused view of risk to a laser-focused view of key risks that impact strategy and goals. Quantifying the value of ERM as a whole is the sum total of the value derived across the enterprise from those individually focused efforts.

ERM is a process and a sound management practice. One of its outputs is information. Properly implemented, an ERM program helps identify elements in a business plan or strategy that are worthy of additional analysis before decisions are made or plans are executed. It asks:

- What has been missed?
- Does anyone know or has anyone thought about all the risks?
- What level of confidence is needed to move forward with this strategy?

A true value of ERM, then, is that it provides management with a method for reducing the uncertainty of decisions.

What Is Meant by "Measuring the Value of ERM"?

The value of a process is measured by the resulting financial or other types of benefits the organization derives from the process. For example, business process reengineering (BPR) focuses on improving the quality of business processes so that the base benefits, such as gained efficiency or growth, are heightened.

As ERM is a process the resulting benefits should be measurable.

Simply put, ERM is a process of identifying risk related to business goals or objectives and mitigating that risk. If we can quantify the amount of risk that has been reduced, or the opportunity uncovered, we can claim that ERM as a process has a quantified value.

In order to measure the value of ERM, it is necessary to measure the magnitude of the risk. If we have a lack of knowledge or confidence about the outcome of a situation and there is a possibility the outcome will result in a loss, we have risk. If we can establish the level of uncertainty, i.e. there is a 50/50 chance of failure, and we can quantify the potential loss, e.g. the company could lose $5M if the plan fails, then we can determine the value of ERM if it is able to reduce that loss.

Measuring

What does it mean to measure something? In his book **How to Measure Anything**, Douglas Hubbard describes measurement as a quantitatively expressed reduction of uncertainty based on one or more observations.[1] He goes on to say if you can observe anything, you can observe more or less of it, and a measurement is valuable no matter how fuzzy if it tells you more than you knew before. It follows, then, that if ERM can be shown to have value, then that value can be measured.

While not ignoring the soft benefits of the process, if ERM can reduce the uncertainty of business decisions, then the ERM process is of high value. So, when we are talking about measuring ERM in this chapter, we are talking about measuring or quantifying how much of the uncertainty surrounding the achievement of the strategy has been reduced. Based on Hubbard's definition of measurement, any information discovered during the process of analyzing the risk that reduces the uncertainty about the ability of a strategy to succeed or the ability to execute the strategy effectively is of value and can be measured.

Quantitatively measuring the value of ERM is essentially measuring the value of the information that is generated by the ERM process. While it may be difficult to describe the value of ERM in one broad measure, it is possible to measure the value as it relates to a specific strategy. The collective value of the information generated for each specific strategy element can be summarized. Measuring the value of ERM, then, is measuring the collective value of that information.

To do that, it is necessary to view and measure the components of information that are generated by the ERM process.

An ERM process should begin with an analysis of the business plan or strategy. Each of the individual strategy elements will comprise many decisions, actions, and executions that typically involve multiple functional units within the organization as a whole. The ERM process should help identify the risks that can impact any of those elements. Those risks should be analyzed based on established categories to ensure completeness, and those categories should be broken down and related to the individual business functions so that the risk can be understood and acted upon.

Before starting to measure ERM or the collective value of any of the components of information it will generate, ask what part of the strategy the reduction of uncertainty (measurement) will benefit most. In other words, what really matters the most?

Quite often people jump right into the process of broadly identifying and analyzing risk. They will begin the process by developing a risk catalog or listing of all the possible risks the organization may face, and they end up spending a lot of time evaluating risks that just don't matter. If the risks that are being evaluated are of little or no importance to the strategy, then any measurement or reduction of uncertainty about such risks will be of little value to the strategy. As a result the ERM process will be considered of little or no value. Approaching risk identification in this manner will result in the ultimate failure of the ERM because there will have been no way to determine its value other than as a means of providing a list of all the risks the company faces.

How to Measure the Value of ERM

Before we begin, these questions should be asked:

- Which specific strategy will this measurement reduce uncertainty for?

- How much is already known about what is going to be measured?

- Is it of value to reduce the uncertainty for this strategy?

> "Even though 'risk' and 'uncertainty' are frequently dismissed as immeasurable, they are aspects of almost any conceivable decision model one could make, especially for the "big" decisions in life and business."
>
> —Douglas Hubbard[2]

Risk is measurable uncertainty. If we can measure the risk, we can measure the reduction of risk. If we can measure the reduction of risk, we can quantitatively measure the value of ERM.

As with seeking an answer for most things, we need to start by asking the right questions. The process of risk identification starts by breaking down the strategy.

- How much is already known?

- What are the most important strategies?

- How much value will they bring to the organization?

- What are the risks that affect these strategies?

- Have all of the risks been identified?

- How much is known about those risks?

By stepping through the process in this manner, the most important strategies are easily indentified. Once the most valuable strategies are identified, the most important questions become:

- How much uncertainty is there within this specific strategy?

- Is there confidence about its success?

- Have all the risks been thought through?

- How much uncertainty is there about the identified risks?

If we ask the right questions, we are likely to uncover additional questions or variables that need to be considered before the decision to execute the strategy moves forward.

The value of ERM can be determined by how much information is uncovered and how much that information reduces the uncertainty about a decision—or, if ways to reduce the risk are identified, how much the potential success of the strategy will be improved.

For example, one of the key strategies in the Curation Inc. case study in *Enterprise Risk Management: Straight to the Point* was a realignment of the sales force to focus on existing accounts as opposed to new business.

The proposed strategy was projected to increase overall sales by 15%, from $290M to $333M. Intuitively everyone knew that focusing the sales force on clients where Curation already had a strong relationship was a good idea. Many highly reliable consultants stated and popular sales theory indicated that a focus on existing clients significantly increased cross-selling, protected against competition, and improved team selling efforts, which had to result in increased revenue.

When identifying risk in the strategy by evaluating it across established risk categories, however, one item emerged in the industry/marketplace risk category. A question was asked about whether or not existing customers were willing to spend an additional 15% on the services that Curation offered.

While researching this question, a seemingly unrelated article surfaced about a slowdown in infrastructure development in China. While none of their major customers had direct involvement with building cities in China, many of Curation's customers had customers who did. A further analysis of spending projections within the customer base revealed that on average most customers would only buy 3–5% more in services than they currently did unless there was an upturn in the economic environment in China or some other part of the world. An analysis of previous years' revenues revealed that business from new customers was historically in the range of 4–7% almost regardless of worldwide construction activities. That meant that the expected increase in revenue of $43M (15%) might be as little as $5.8M, whereas the increase in new business revenue could be as high as $20.3M.

The value of the information developed by the ERM process then was a range of as much as $14.5M (the most that could be realistically expected by shifting a focus to existing customers) or as low as a loss of $3M (should the sales team have been able to generate the additional 5% by focusing on existing clients vs. the low end of historic sales to new clients of 4%).

The initial level of uncertainty regarding this strategy was low, so the value of the ERM process appeared to be meager. But by asking the right questions and uncovering the industry/marketplace risk, Curation changed their level of uncertainty. It was now much higher than it was before the analysis. Due to the ERM process, Curation was able to reevaluate the cost of the sales force realignment in the light of a more realistic projection of potential sales.

The true value of the information generated by the ERM process could be calculated in terms of the savings or expenditures related to the sales force realignment.

The ERM process had a tangible value in resetting sales expectations, which if missed may have had an impact on market perceptions and resulting shareholder value.

The moral of the story is that if the uncertainty about a strategy is truly low and we know and understand all the risks involved, then the value of ERM may be low. But if there is a high degree of uncertainty, then the value derived from the ERM process will be high.

To summarize the approach, begin by asking some basic questions:

- What risk categories relate to the strategy item under review?
- How much is known about the risk category as related to the strategy?
- Is an expert opinion needed?
- How does uncertainty create risk for the decision?
- Will additional information make the company alter its course?

In order to measure the value of ERM as a whole, we need to measure the value of individual components. As in the above example, the focus was on one element of one identified risk that would have an effect on the overall sales strategy.

In fact, the specific element in the example above was only one across the full range of risk categories that needed to be evaluated. Each strategy element or tactic needs to be evaluated against all the risk categories to determine what risks exist within each category.

Non-Strategic Measures

In addition to measuring the impact of ERM on strategic aspects of the business, we can measure some basic operational aspects. See the chart following for some examples.

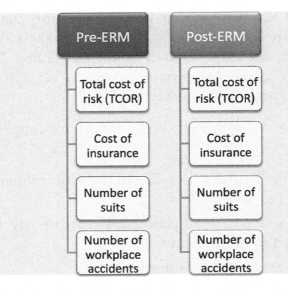

Measurement Techniques

There is no such thing as absolute certainty. The value of measurement is in its ability to reduce the amount of uncertainty about an issue. Consider the volume of the ocean. We can come close, but will never be able to say, with absolute certainty, what that volume is. We may come up with a number that may suit our purpose however, such as estimating expected changes in sea levels based on climate change when planning to build on land close to the shore.

If we can reduce our uncertainty, we can make better decisions. Even if we are able to reduce our uncertainty only by a small degree, that may be better than making a decision blindly. If we can improve our knowledge about the possible outcome of a strategy, even if that knowledge brings us only a little closer to certainty, it is better than setting a strategy or making a decision with less information.

It is likely that while evaluating risk across a broad range of categories we will encounter areas that do not lend themselves to hard facts.

While there may be many areas of business where hard numbers are available, such as in financial areas, there are many areas, especially when related to risk, that are less concrete. Risk factors in categories such as the geopolitical environment, talent management, and reputation may not always lend themselves to hard factual data.

In *Enterprise Risk Management: Straight to the Point*, ERM Process Point 2 described establishing scales for the enterprise. In many cases the scales could not be related to an actual number. In those areas, we may have had to rely on ranges or estimates. When we need to rely on ranges, those ranges may not be linear in nature. When using a scale of 1–5 for example, 4 is more than 3, but not necessarily twice as much as 2. The number 4 simply means greater than 3, but not as great as 5.

You may also need to measure things based on degree of belief. "I believe New York is closer to Boston than Miami." While not exact, it certainly improves what is known about that distance.

This is a good time to point out that belief, in some cases, may be all we have, but it also may be all we need to know and all the measurement we need to make. We certainly could find out the exact distance between those cities, but if all we are trying to evaluate is the risk of our sales force being able to reach customers in one location sooner than those in another, that may be all we need to know.

There is also value in estimating—for example, bigger than a breadbox, smaller than a house. And while the estimate of one individual may be helpful, an estimate by consensus will likely provide a more accurate number.

There are a number of ways to determine the value of information. One method, developed by Hubbard, is called applied information economics[3]—a calculation of the economic value of the information. His method can easily be applied to ERM as follows:

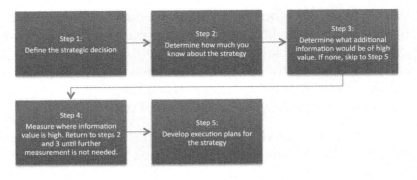

As we mentioned at the beginning of this chapter, there is no magic wand, but ERM can be measured and its value determined. Measuring ERM is not simple, but it does not need to be complex.

Once it is determined what is to be measured, it is necessary to decide on one or more methods of measurement.

Let us take reputational risk as an example. How do you measure the risk, and how much it will affect a strategy? Few companies have an exact number that indicates the state of their reputation, although there are soft numbers that can be used as rough approximates, such as public opinion polls, customer satisfaction surveys, and social media indicators.

Again, always begin with the strategy.

- Does the strategy in question have any risk of tarnishing the company's reputation?
- What will happen or why should we care if the company's reputation is tarnished?
  - o Will it result in a loss of referrals?
  - o Will customers be lost?
  - o Will it affect our credit rating resulting in the increase cost of capital?
  - o Will it affect our share value?

o Will advertisers be lost?

o Will key partners be lost?

o Will key staff be lost?

o All of the above?

The interesting aspect of all of the above impact possibilities is that they are, in fact, very meaningful and very measureable. Although there is no single comprehensive and objective way to measure reputation, there is a way to measure each of the aforementioned impacts. You need to break down what needs to be measured into what can be measured.

- What is the value of a referral, and can it be estimated how many referrals will be lost?

- How many new customers are typically added during a defined time period?

- What is our belief about how many customers that could be lost?

- What's our current cost of capital, and how much will an increase affect the bottom line?

- How much will a decline in stock price affect shareholders?

- How much ad revenue might be lost?

- What is the cost of replacing key staff?

It is undeniable that each of these issues can be measured. The question is, by what method?

Using your Intuition for Measurement

Using your intuition is essentially a qualitative approach to measurement. But if the objective is to reduce the amount of uncertainty of a decision, adding any qualitative measurements to quantitative results will only improve the outcome of the measurement process. It might be good, however, to validate that intuition with other members of the decision team, or even credible individuals who are not associated with the decision at all. At a minimum, it can validate that intuition. At a maximum, it can clarify the intuitive thought.

Simple Observations

This is a perfect example of why and how to involve all levels of staff in both the identification and the analysis of risk issues, as we described in chapter 3. Operational staff are eyes on the ground. While they may not have detailed statistics about an issue or the risk, they may be able to describe the reality of the situation through observation far better than someone on the outside looking in, especially in the areas of customer behavior, social attitudes, product ease of use (vs. functionality), or other soft risks. The input of those closest to the process can offer insight, essential additional value to the measurement of risk.

This method of measurement may also be useful if we wanted to know if changes made to a given process or product would make a difference. Would anyone notice the difference? If not, perhaps the mitigation process has no value.

It may also be useful to recognize that it may only be possible to reduce a risk rather than eliminate it—for example, in terms of criticisms posted on social media.

Perhaps the simplest method of measurement is observation. Yogi Berra is famously alleged to have said, "You can observe a lot just by watching."

Making basic, thoughtfully designed observations can go a long way to establishing an element of measurement that may be useful in measuring risk and the result of reducing it. For example, if you work in a restaurant or a theater or any business that caters to the public, you can observe an increase in patronage or attendance. Most good businesses will have a method of determining revenue per customer. If your normal revenue per customer is X, you can easily calculate the impact of a loss of 10% of your customers as X × 0.10 due to some risk.

But how do you know how many customers you will lose?

- Are there past issues that resulted in a reputational loss?

- Has any other company in your industry experience a loss of customers based on taking a similar risk?

- Could a consensus opinion be formed by members of your risk committee or the executive committee?

If the risk is demonstrably reduced and the actual loss of customer patronage with its concomitant loss of revenue is computed, the value of ERM is explicit. The key is to break down what is to be measured into the smallest and most easily identifiable metric at your disposal.

When you add up the cost of the risk (or the impact) using the broken-down elements of your analysis, the value of the ERM process will essentially be how much this cost could be reduced by either a change in strategy or by the development of mitigation plans.

Breaking the Problem Down into Measurable Components

The best way to get to some means of measuring the value of the process and the related risk is to break the question down into what is obviously measureable. For example, will a particular change in an HR policy or practice result in a reduction in turnover, minimizing legal liability, or reducing an insurance premium? If a risk mitigation action will facilitate any of these things, then determine by how much. If an estimate can be determined, then the value of the mitigation process can be postulated and actually measured over time.

Just about anything can be broken down to something that has a number associated with it.

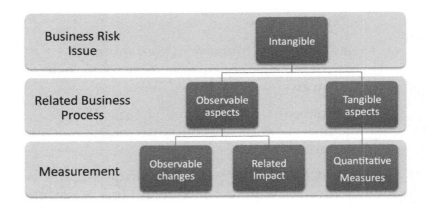

Consideration of Prior Information

There are few business functions that are so unique that no historical information can be obtained about their operations or results. Dynamic risk deduction[4] looks at the business environment within which the risks exist, and includes such areas as:

- Past issues/risks faced by the functional area

- Impending political/regulatory changes and trends

- Impending socioeconomic changes and trends

- Potential trends from one egregious occurrence

- Benchmark data

Each of these areas of focus will or should have quantifiable dimensions. The quantitative factors related to the risk and the associated mitigation processes can be measured and the quantitative value of each determined.

Using Very Simple Statistical Techniques

For most business processes these days, some quantitative modeling process surely exists. With the vast amount of big data and the processing power available today, it is likely that a statistical model can be applied to just about anything. But at what cost and with what level of complexity?

Fortunately, you can often get a reasonable approximation of statistical results by simply refining or enhancing human judgment.

This process is often referred to as the "sniff test." If you stop and think through a situation, how much do you inherently know? How much can be determined by simple estimates or judgment given the facts at hand?

In reality, if you try to do this on your own, in an area you are familiar with, you are likely to be short sighted and more than likely biased.

A study conducted by Michael Mauboussin considered the intuitive input of a group of his students and showed that by using the input of a diverse group, the risk of any business objective, its level of inherent risk, and the effectiveness of planned mitigation will be brought to the surface.[5] The process of vetting such issues across a broad spectrum of smart people both inside and external to the organization will bring out issues and allow a means of measuring the value of managing its risk.

The bottom line is that if an important strategy has a lot of associated uncertainty, even a marginal reduction of the uncertainty will have significant value.

As described in Hubbard's ***How to Measure Anything***, the process may include the following elements:

- What is the expected value of the strategy?

  - o Quantitative value

  - o Qualitative value

- How much could the value be reduced by unmitigated risk (uncertainty)?

- What is the current estimated level of uncertainty?

- What is the value of addition information

- What measures (mitigations) are in place that might reduce the uncertainty and therefore preserve the value of the strategy?

- What new measure could be put in place?

- What is the cost of the mitigation?

- What is the extent of the value that has been preserved (value of the strategy less the cost of mitigation), or, essentially, what is the value of the ERM process?

Quantifying the Value of Information

If we could quantify the value of the information ERM provides, we would probably spend more time measuring risks that mattered and less time on risks that don't. If a particular risk, no matter how potentially devastating it may seem, has little or no value to any major business strategy or objective, then why bother to measure it?

For example, hurricanes are pretty devastating things. A major hurricane can cause severe damage to people and property. A severe hurricane could have a devastating impact on IT capabilities, supply chain and business operations.

But if you are identifying and measuring the risk related to a marketing strategy, the potential affect of a hurricane may not be worth measuring. Always ask the question, is what is being measured important to the specific strategy in question?

Graphic Measurement

While it is important to calculate the value of each individual component of the ERM process, at times it may be interesting to look at the value of the process as a whole.

In the case study detailed in ***Enterprise Risk Management: Straight to the Point***, we showed what might have looked like a classic risk heat map.[6] It was in fact very different from a typical risk heat map that shows the likelihood and impact of one risk as compared to other identified risk. Heat maps of this nature may be useful if your primary objective is to place an emphasis on and focus on what may be calculated to be the top risk by either internal company analysis or some industry-developed list.

Heat maps that focus only on the risk, however, are not as useful if your primary objective is ensure the success of company-specific strategies, goals, and objectives. In that case a very different heat map is required.

In the case study, the management team began by identifying the current year's business strategy and determining what the most important goals and objectives were. The management team proceeded to identify the risks, on a function-by-function basis, that could inhibit the success of individual important strategy items and thus inhibit the success of the strategy as a whole.

The result of that process was a heat map that plotted which individual strategy element was at the greatest risk of success, not simply which individual risk was the greatest.

The resulting heat map looked like this:

Business Strategies At-Risk

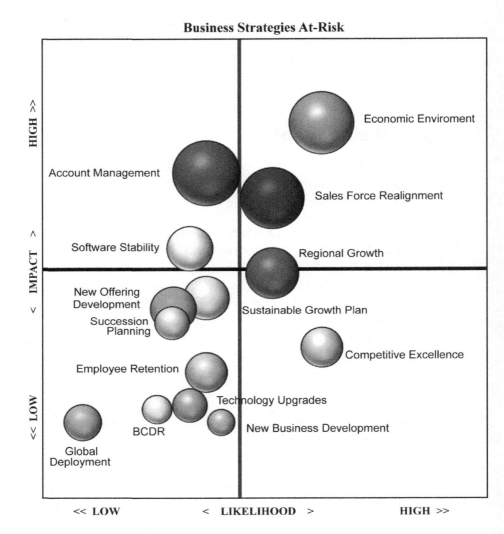

It is important to note that the items listed are not business risks, but business strategies. This heat map was designed to enable management to pay attention to the business strategies that are at greatest risk of failure, rather than simply to focus on an issue that was determined to be a high-risk but might relate only to a lower-priority strategy item.

In short, the map was designed to direct management's attention to areas of the business they needed to be worried about the most.

This heat map, however, is the after-risk mitigation map. What was not shown in the case study was the before-mitigation chart. The before chart looked like this:

Business Strategies At-Risk Prior to Risk Mitigation Processes

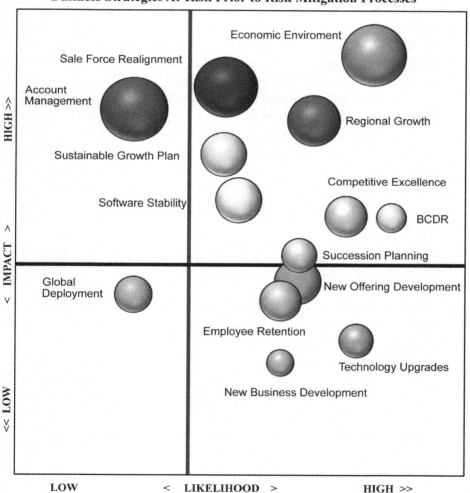

The before picture looks a bit more grim than the after picture. The difference, of course, is that this is the view of business strategies before mitigation strategies were developed and applied. There are no business strategies in the low-risk quadrant and at least five top strategies that are either solidly in or touching the high-risk quadrant. Ultimately, through proper mitigation, many of the strategies moved out of the high-risk quadrant into the lower-risk quadrants or into the very low-risk portion of the map.

Although these maps do not display an exact overall value of the ERM process, they do show the value in terms of overall improvement of the company's chance of any given strategy succeeding. For example, one of the strategies that was most at risk, Regional Growth, moved from the high-risk quadrant towards the middle of the map, thus showing it has a much improved chance of succeeding. It also identifies the Economic Environment as remaining a high-risk issue still having the most significant risk. By highlighting this issue, senior management and the board can focus their attention on what is most significant from a risk perspective.

There are, of course, numbers underlying the charts, and these numbers are the result of breaking down the related issues into measureable components.

The position of the strategy item on the map (shown by the bubble) is a plot of the point of intersection of likelihood and impact. The size of the bubble is simply the mathematical result of multiplying the likelihood times the impact. The numerical size of the bubble, while a measurement, is essentially meaningless other than to graphically show the overall magnitude of the risks facing one business strategy element relative to some other business strategy element. The higher the risk and the higher the impact, the larger the bubble.

For example, the sales force realignment plan was identified as a major factor in the success of the overall business plan.

A number of strategies were quite complex, and given it was going to be a very tough year, it was important to determine if any risk that might cause the sales force realignment to suffer could lead to any of the other strategies failing. Although this may sound like a normal state of affairs, a number of external factors, such as the current economic environment, the status of the potential IPO, the experience level of the executives, and other factors might impact the resolve and abilities of the management team. Thus, successful realignment of the sales force became a key factor in the execution of the plan and worthy of examination in light of the risks that might cause that performance to suffer.

The value of the ERM process was shown visually as the position of any given strategy item moving from the red zone of the heat map to the yellow or green zone of the map.

The evaluation consisted of determining the likelihood and impact tolerance of risk factors and the effect on business results. The scores were determined by the executive team based on the following scoring criteria.

The likelihood of a risk factor occurring was scored from 1 to 5 based on the following criteria:

Score	Time frame	Frequency	Intensity
5	Immediately	Very often	At its highest level
4	3 months	Often	Very high level
3	12 months	Periodically	Increasing level
2	30 months	Occasionally	Normal level
1	60 months	Rarely	Low level

The impact of a risk factor was scored from 1 to 5 based on the following criteria:

Impact tolerance scale	5	4	3	2	1
Revenue erosion	100%	75%	50%	25%	<10%
Fines and penalties	>$1M	$500K	$250K	$100K	<$25K
Cost of op- erations	>20%	10%	5%	2%	<1%
Days of downtime	>30	10	5	2	1
Reputation impact (# customers lost)	15	10	5	2	1

The method used in developing these scores was based on Mauboussin's approach as described previously in this chapter. The averages are used to develop the points and bubble sizes on the charts for a before-and-after view of the value.

Chapter 5

The Value of Applying ERM to Corporate Strategy

The board, CEO, senior team, and others provide input for the company's strategic plan. The board and CEO are charged with making the final decision about the strategic direction of the organization. In the normal course of business, a strategic plan gets memorialized in a strategic plan document that is shared, more or less completely, with employees and other key stakeholders.

What Is Strategy, and Where Does It Fit within the ERM Process?

Strategy is essentially the description of and roadmap to the destination that company wants to reach. The ERM process starts with a deep understanding of the strategy and the strategic goals and objectives. The next step in the process is identifying major uncertainties associated with the strategy and goals. In other words, what risks are likely to get in the way of their achievement? Then risks are quantified and qualified (in terms of their likelihood and impact), prioritized, and paired with mitigation plans. Depending on the risks identified, there may need to be an adjustment to the strategy, goals, or objectives.

There is an intersection between the ERM process and the strategic planning process that is worthy of note. One of the popular constructs that strategists use is called a SWOT analysis. SWOT stands for strengths, weaknesses, opportunities, and threats. By analyzing each of these, an organization can build unique responses to better use their strengths, shore up their weaknesses, capitalize on their opportunities, and avoid or minimize their threats.

Threats, like risks or uncertainties, are potential inhibitors to reaching goals. They may be current or emerging, they may or may not fully materialize, and their impact may be difficult to quantify. Regardless, they cannot be ignored.

The threat analysis, in particular, is a clear point where strategy and ERM intersect. The threats identified as part of the SWOT and the risks identified as part of the ERM process augment each other.

Each organization needs to determine its own logical time frames for beginning and ending a particular process cycle as well as for renewing the cycle on some periodic basis. Provision needs to be made to insert significant new risks that become known between the end of one process cycle and the beginning of the next. Factors to consider in developing the time frame for establishing an ERM process cycle include when strategic planning takes place, when resources are available to participate in the process, and when the senior team and board of directors meet to consider strategy and risk management.

Following is an overview of the ERM process as a flowchart. As with most processes it is iterative. That is because strategies change, risks morph, new risks emerge, and some risks disappear.

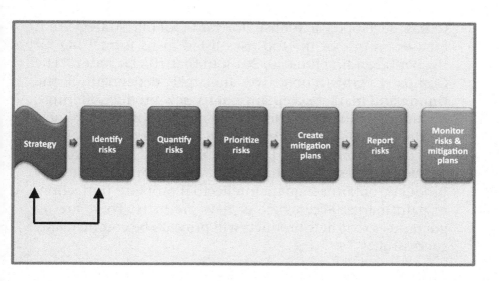

An Example of Alignment between Strategy and ERM

3M is a large, global company with many product lines—for example, healthcare, office products, and personal safety. It has been in business for more than one hundred years. Its age does not guarantee future success, though. Many companies with long histories finally succumbed by disappearing altogether in bankruptcy or by being subsumed into a stronger competitor. A couple of notable examples of companies with very long histories that have failed in recent decades include Bethlehem Steel (with roots back to 1857) and Washington Mutual Savings Bank (founded as Washington National Building Loan and Investment Association in 1889).

We have no inside knowledge about the deliberations or workings of 3M. From a review of public information, it appears as though 3M's current management understands that no company can rest on what has gone before. The risk of an outdated strategy or obsolescent products seems to be well recognized.

It has developed a robust, forward-looking strategy that focuses on one of the top risks listed in its form 10-Q for the period ending June 30, 2013. In that 10-Q it states: "The Company's growth objectives are largely dependent on the timing and market acceptance of its new product offerings, including its ability to continually renew its pipeline of new products and to bring those products to market. This ability may be adversely affected by difficulties or delays in product development, such as the inability to identify viable new products, obtain adequate intellectual property protection, or gain market acceptance of new products. There are no guarantees that new products will prove to be commercially successful."[1]

This risk is one that is faced by all companies, especially in today's dynamic marketplace. Each will respond to it in different ways or not at all. Some will not respond simply because they have not recognized the risk or the magnitude of the risk. 3M has chosen to tackle it head-on with a bold strategic thrust. Here is how 3M's CEO, Inge Thulin, describes the company's major strategic thrust in response to this risk:

> The labs are a beehive of activity, and they are about to get even busier. Over the next five years, 3M will sharply increase dollars spent on research and development, as the race to create new and better products becomes ever more global and competitive.
>
> I believe that what is driving this company in terms of return for us is the investment in research and development, and every time we do it we know that we have a competitive advantage.
>
> The goal: to increase the number of new products the company creates and, just as importantly, gets onto store shelves.

Generating revenue from groundbreaking science isn't a foregone conclusion.

3M is so singularly focused on making sure science moves from invention to mass production, that the company has an internal measure called the 'NPVI,' or New Product Vitality Index. The NPVI is the percentage of revenue the company generates from products that didn't exist five years earlier.

In 2008, 25 percent of the company's revenue came from products created in the last five years. Today, that number is 34 percent.

That's an incredible figure. We are $30 billion in terms of revenue as a company; meaning over $10 billion of the products we are selling today did not exist five years ago. I wonder if anyone else can say the same.[2]

The article goes on to say that Thulin expects that number to reach 40% by 2017 with the increase in R&D.

Again, most, if not all, companies have the same risk regarding the need to innovate and create new products. This risk stems from the exponential increase in the power of technology to transform products, the competition's race to incorporate such technology, the public's demand for novel or more technologically savvy products, and the changing dynamics in the regulatory, environmental, and social arenas. Indeed, many companies have also established a goal of reaching a certain percentage of revenue from products introduced in the last three or five years.

The things that make 3M stand out in addressing this risk include:

- Taking the risk seriously
- Building a strategy with goals that addresses the risk

- Nurturing a culture of innovation

- Creating the right infrastructure to support innovation—for example, their labs

- Supporting the labs and other key functions with budgets that enable them to innovate products that can be commercialized

- Talking about this aspect of strategy internally and externally, thereby reinforcing it

- Developing a performance management system, including rewards, that is synchronized with the strategy

All companies need to recognize, on the other hand, that there is risk in introducing new products: Will the product resonate with the intended customer group? Will it perform as advertised? Has it been priced appropriately? These and other questions are critical. The insurance industry is very interesting in this regard. The core of its business is accepting risk. But when an insurer offers a new product, especially related to an emerging risk area, there are enormous uncertainties. For example, when cyber coverage first came out there were risks around whether the underwriters would know enough about the types of losses that may occur, what precedents the courts will set in deciding cyber-related suits, and how well underwriters could evaluate the level of security that the insured had built into their systems, networks, policies, and practices. Yet, innovation in insurance has not abated. Rather, it has increased with the creation of all sorts of cyber coverage, supply chain coverage, and even some reputational coverages.

Attributes of Strategic Risks

Some strategic risks are common across industries, some are unique to certain industries, and some are unique to a particular company. The leader of the ERM process, together with the leader of the strategic planning process, should work with senior management in order to identify the significant risks that the company's strategic thinking must account for, whether the company is moving forward with a momentum strategy or a new strategy. In a small company this may all be the responsibility of the CEO or CFO or someone to whom they delegate these responsibilities.

Strategic risks may be facing the company in its current state or may emerge as a result of a changed strategy. They may appear as a result of the transition or transformation between the old and new strategies. All of these must be considered.

New internally generated risks

New externally generated risks

The strategy must take into account all the key risks

Changing current risks

Strategic risk:

- May stand in the way of achieving strategy

- May be significant enough to impact the achievement of strategy in a meaningful way

- May be macro in nature—that is, emanate from a national or global phenomenon

- Conversely, may emanate from a company-specific strategic, cultural, or operational condition

The Need to Think Big

A company has to think big when considering strategic risks. The question to ask is, what is happening, or is about to happen, that will radically challenge the company's ability to remain a going concern given the established direction?

Some examples of specific big-picture questions include:

- Is there a risk that some new technology will make our product(s) unnecessary? Consider buggy whips, typewriters, and travel agents.

- Is there a risk that demographic or cultural changes beginning to take shape could make our products undesirable to current and prospective customers? Consider suspenders and dress hats.

- Is there a risk that economic conditions will worsen and disproportionally hurt our assets or our customers? Consider luxury condo developers, airplane leasing companies.

- Is there a risk that our financial position is too heavily leveraged to withstand a sharp downturn in the market and could lead to an illiquid state? Consider Bear Stearns, Swissair.

- Is there a risk that looming laws or regulations will make our products too expensive or undesirable? Consider cigarettes, NYC Big Gulp drinks.

- Is there a risk that the company will take a reputational hit that will result in a complete lack of stakeholder trust? Consider Arthur Andersen, Washington Mutual.

- Is there a risk that our competitors can overtake us completely because they have been able to positively differentiate themselves but our company has not? Consider Circuit City Inc., Orion Pictures.

- Is there a risk that the political or climate conditions in countries our company has decided to generate revenue from (or get our finished products or raw material from) will deteriorate to the point of causing us financial injury? Consider the 2012 Japanese tsunami and the 2012 political uprisings around the world.

- Is there a risk that the culture that our strategy espouses or the governance level our company has adopted is not sufficient to stop a rogue or misguided employee before he or she causes serious financial harm or ruin? Consider Barings Bank, the London Whale.

- Is there a risk that a major change in our strategy will not resonate with customers or will not be able to be implemented by staff only experienced in the old ways of doing business? Consider JC Penney.

It is not only the questions that are important, of course. The answer to the questions can enable a company to create or hone its strategy for winning in the marketplace. If management responds in a superficial or haphazard way, then the outcome will not be good. Worse yet, if management puts its proverbial head in the sand, the strategy could be doomed. A prerequisite for having a meaningful risk assessment of the strategy is to have knowledgeable and open-minded senior executives involved in the discussion.

Some Potential Disruptive Technologies on the Horizon

Right now, standing in the wings are a number potentially disruptive technologies. They are real. Some have been commercialized to some extent, while are others are in test mode.

Among these are:

- **Driverless cars**: These could impact industries as diverse as insurers, driver's education schools, auto manufacturers, software developers and wireless communications companies.

- **3D printing:** This could impact manufacturers of all kinds, distributors of all kinds, and raw material suppliers at minimum.

- **The Internet of things:** This could impact manufacturers of all kinds and people in all professions.

- **Personal aircraft (drones):** These could impact logistics companies, governments, builders, and urban planners.

- **Genomics:** This could impact healthcare, law firms, and people of all walks of life.

Identifying Strategic Risks

As difficult as it may be to spot the strategic risks to a specific company, there are techniques that can be helpful in this quest.

Review the Strategy against Risk Categories

Take each main category of potential risk and determine what is happening within it that might create risk for the vision or strategies that have been planned. Because there are so many categories of risk, it is useful to work with a limited, high-level set, as described in *Enterprise Risk Management: Straight to the Point*:

- Economic/financial markets

- Legal/regulatory

- Geopolitical

- Marketplace/competition

- Customer demographics

- Technology advancement

- Cyber

- Operations

- Talent

- Natural environment

Extrapolate from a Changing Market Landscape

Look at what is already obviously changing in the company's market space—for example, new competitors, supplier issues, customer preference changes—to determine whether these pose a threat to your strategy. Everyone knows that risk comes in all shapes and sizes. A customer preference-related risk could be that everyone starts to want a company's product but they are not ready with enough inventory. A risk inspired by a positive reaction is often overlooked but can have very negative effects if it turns customers against the company through disappointment or annoyance.

Disintermediation has been a risk trend in the marketplace for the past several decades. The history of travel agents, stockbrokers, and others who have been replaced by the Internet or Internet aggregators is still fresh and ongoing. Another form of disintermediation risk comes about when a company's distributor becomes a manufacturer and provider. For example, flashlight apps sold via smartphones became unnecessary when smartphones incorporated a flashlight feature.

Thus, it is necessary to keep a sharp eye on the market, look at risk from positive and negative points of view (what happens if the business is more or less successful than planned?) and be ready to adapt, change, or innovate out of a risk that has materialized and will do severe damage.

Learn from the Past

Sometimes risk scenarios repeat themselves because the underlying cause of the risk may have abated but may not have been eliminated. The lack of transparency in the insurance arena regarding large regional and global broker compensation became a crisis in recent times, both in the 1990s and again in the early 2000s. The second time, brokers and carriers spent large amounts of time of money as they decided how to address the issue, changed processes and communications protocol, and assured regulators and customers that transparency was being achieved. Had the risk been fully mitigated the first time around, the second round of expending time and money as well as damaging trust would not have occurred.

From a strategic point of view, the brokerage that addressed this risk in a customer-centric and breakthrough way when it first appeared could have outcompeted the others.

Note the First Warning Signal of a Risk Trend

As soon as Amazon started to reach critical mass as just a bookseller, that was the time for all booksellers to take a look at their strategy to decide whether their current business model could withstand a growing shift in customer buying patterns.

Barnes and Noble appears to have taken note of the risk to their model fairly quickly when they cut down on brick and mortar expansion, introduced their own e-reader (Nook), and introduced a loyalty program that customers had to pay to join, thus creating stickiness. Borders, on the other hand, continued to expand their physical footprint, did not innovate in the e-reader space, and offered a free loyalty program, which is more of a commodity store play.

How fast and far companies are able to go to address these existential risks will be what separates the winners from the losers.

Review SEC Filings and Other Public Documents of Competitors

It may well be that competitors or other companies are noting a risk that your company has failed to identify. Reviewing the SEC filings, especially section 1A, "Risk Factors," of the 10-Ks of competitors or other companies of your size or in your geographies may help to pinpoint areas of risk that you are also exposed to. Although the disclosure is often fairly superficial and generic, some companies are more forthcoming than others in what they choose to disclose.

Discuss the Risk Landscape with Strategists, Risk Professionals, and Academics

No matter how objective or informed a management team thinks it is, there will always be the danger of being too myopic to see the bigger picture and recognize all the threats. Discussing the risk landscape in a confidential way with others who are not too close to your own organization but are well informed enhances the ability to identify risks.

Numerous studies show how problem solving is improved when a diverse group of people contributes to the solution. We posit that the same is true of identifying risks. Each person will come to the identification process with a different set of knowledge and experience, a unique way of looking at the marketplace, and a greater or lesser ability to see connections, interrelationships, and trend lines from which to spot current and emerging risks.

Identifying Strategic Risk

During 2013, several for-profit providers of adult education publicly announced issues relating to reduced enrollment and suits against them for various practices. One large, well known organization, of this type, was especially hard hit. According to the Associated Press, in October 2013, " Strayer Education Inc. shares plunged Thursday after the for-profit education company reported that its net income fell 17 percent on a drop in enrollment. It also said it would cut its workforce by 20 percent and close 20 physical schools, further lowering its enrollment."[3]

Any risk that could have a significant impact on share price or income can be classified a strategic risk. When organizations in this educational sector do strategic planning, it would be good for them to consider risk related questions such as:

- Is there something happening in the economic, societal or other sphere that could have a material impact on enrollments?

- What are our own trend lines telling us about enrollments?

- What are all the risk factors associated with growing physical locations? Are there alternatives?

- What ways can we reduce the risk of students being unable to afford tuition such as future potential employer corporate sponsorships, scholarships from outside foundations, extended payment plans?

To further illustrate the thought process that leads to a set of questions an organization such as this could ask, see the following:

Identify the risks to key aspects of the strategy and derive questions from them — Strategic Goal: X level of enrollment in X, Y, Z years	What is the risk that enrollment will slacken? What is the most recent enrollment trend line? How is enrollment trending at other adult learning institutions? What do the dropout rate trend lines look like? Have surveys been done of existing and/or potential students?

Identify the risks to the business in general, and derive questions from them — Business Plan Goal: maintain X tuition pricing levels for sufficient margins	What is the risk that students will not be able to pay at current or higher tuition levels? What is happening in the student loan arena, shrinking capacity, growing capacity? What is happening relative to employment/wages of likely students? Have surveys been done of exisiting and/or potential students?

The Value of ERM Relative to Strategy

Given that company collapses are so often caused by failed strategies—either badly conceived or poorly executed— the tremendous value of ERM should be clear. ERM's main focus is on finding and steering clear of or mitigating the risks to the strategy. It is not enough necessarily to address the risks to strategy; it may be that the strategy itself has to be revised. In essence, strategy development and ERM are interrelated and inform each other.

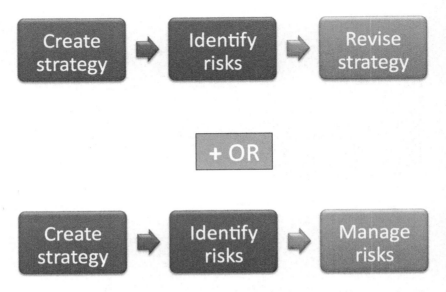

One of the somewhat unexpected benefits that ERM practitioners are finding is the ability to ensure that the organization is truly aligned to strategic goals. When asked about risks to strategy achievement, staff at all levels in many organizations have let it be known in ERM workshops, focus groups, questionnaires, and surveys that they did not know what the strategy and strategic goals were. Or they thought they knew but had it wrong. This allowed the organizations to take the necessary steps to inform or correct the general understanding of where their companies are headed and what needs to be accomplished to get them there.

In summary, ERM adds value to strategy development and implementation by:

- Ensuring that the strategy has been well thought through

- Protecting the company from risks to its stated strategic direction and goals

- Helping ensure that everyone is clear about the company's direction

- Showing stakeholders, such as rating agencies, investors, and others, that the company is more in command of its environment and has a greater potential for meeting its goals

- Giving a structure to an otherwise haphazard approach to dealing with uncertainties surrounding the strategy

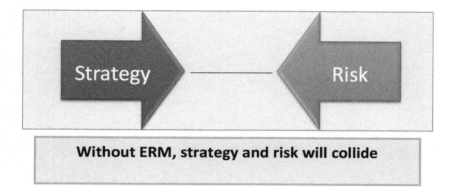

Without ERM, strategy and risk will collide

With ERM, strategy will head off or reduce risk

Chapter 6

The Value of Applying ERM to Mergers and Acquisitions

The acronym M&A refers to both mergers and acquisitions, each of which is distinct and different from the other. A merger is a voluntary combination of two companies into one new legal entity. Thus the companies that have combined their assets and liabilities will dissolve without having to be liquidated. A merger is generally effected by an exchange of pre-merger stock in return for stock of the new company. An acquisition, on the other hand, is taking over controlling interest in a company through a purchase or legal process.

There are many reasons for a company to merge with or acquire another company. Chief among these are to augment organic growth that may or may not be happening in sufficient amounts, to achieve economies of scale such that margins are improved, to take out a competitor that has become too threatening, to avoid looming liquidation, and to enter a new geographic or product market without having to develop it from scratch.

Both mergers and acquisitions involve risk. Risk emanates from the potential for surprises about what the acquired or merged company brings into the new organization. It also stems from the fact that there will need to be actions and changes to accommodate the introduction of one company into another. In addition, there is risk in terms of how the new organization will be perceived by customers, regulators, analysts, and investors, among other stakeholders. Major change is risky. ERM needs to play a key role in M&A activity from the initial idea through implementation and transition.

How Does ERM Play a Role in M&A?

Following is a schematic of ERM within an acquisition transaction, leading to the deal.

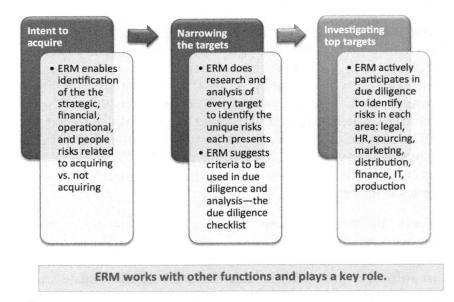

Intent to acquire	Narrowing the targets	Investigating top targets
• ERM enables identification of the the strategic, financial, operational, and people risks related to acquiring vs. not acquiring	• ERM does research and analysis of every target to identify the unique risks each presents • ERM suggests criteria to be used in due diligence and analysis—the due diligence checklist	• ERM actively participates in due diligence to identify risks in each area: legal, HR, sourcing, marketing, distribution, finance, IT, production

ERM works with other functions and plays a key role.

Idea to Acquire

Before a particular acquisition is considered, the chief risk officer, working with the risk committee, should develop a list of the risks that the company faces in doing an acquisition vs. not doing one. The list should comprise risks that conform to the existing conditions. For example:

- The company has no current project management expertise, resulting in a risk that the acquisition will not be handled effectively.
- There is a lack of good targets, resulting in a risk that a poor target will be chosen just to do a deal.

Further, there may be conditions that make it imperative to put risk tolerance parameters in place for the acquisition, and ERM can help with that. For example:

- Long-term debt-to-capital ratio may become too high compared to that of peers post merger/ acquisition and may scare off investors; an increase of 10% may be all the risk that can be tolerated.
- Investors will sell if there is any drop in revenue post merger/acquisition; the risk of a revenue drop cannot be tolerated.

The fact that these risks are surfaced before a potential M&A is under consideration is beneficial because it may induce the company to build some project management expertise or delay until better, more potentially successful candidates are available.

Narrowing Down the Targets

If the acquirer has several potential acquisition targets, there is generally a review of the companies based on publicly available data. The CRO should provide guidance to the acquisition team to ensure that there is risk perspective applied to the available information. High-risk targets should be eliminated or tagged.

The due diligence phase of an acquisition is extremely important. After narrowing down the targets, it will be time to prepare for the phases of the acquisition process, including due diligence. It is never too early to begin to assemble a due diligence plan and checklist. The CRO and/ or ERM committee should be asked to comment on and add to the due diligence list of materials for review and people to interview.

Doing the Due Diligence

The CRO, or whoever is responsible for ERM, also needs to play a role when it comes to the actual due diligence with the acquisition target.

First and foremost, the target's management of risk should be reviewed. How well is risk being managed? What are the top risks? What risks have been shared publicly? Are the identified risks reasonable and comprehensive? Is risk remediation going on, and is it sufficient? How are remediation efforts being monitored?

Second, using an ERM process, the acquirer should develop their own list of potential risks that the target company may bring with it which are not part of its own risk register. These risks could include, for example, financial liabilities that may or may not be readily apparent in the financial statements, negative trending results, key staff who are not willing or able to adapt to new cultures or ways of doing business or systems that may not be fit for purpose within the new combined entity.

Third, the risks stemming from the handling of the acquisition itself should be identified. These risks could include, for example, whether investors will have a basis to sue on the pricing/valuation of the deal, whether employees of the acquired company will have a basis to sue on how they are treated during integration, or whether customers, distributors, and/or suppliers will see a reason to abandon ship based on new ways of doing business that are introduced as part of the acquisition.

An Acquisition Example

Acquisitions consume a great deal of management time before, during, and after the deal has been executed. In addition, they entail frictional costs running the gamut from integrating acquired employees into HR systems and benefits all the way to creating and sending special communications to various stakeholder groups. Very importantly, there are often expenses associated with surprises or unintended consequences. Another type of cost is opportunity cost. During the time that management is dealing with an acquisition (a troubled one or a smooth one), other opportunities, such as new product launches, strategic partnerships, and potentially better acquisition targets, are usually not able to be pursued also.

A great deal has been written about the 1990s acquisition of Snapple by Quaker Oats. Quaker bought Snapple for $1.7 billion in 1994 and sold it to Triarc in 1997 for $300 million.[1]

Thus, the difference in price between what Quaker Oats bought and sold Snapple for is only the tip of the iceberg in terms of what it lost.

Today, Quaker Oats is owned by PepsiCo. Some have said that the acquisition of Snapple led to its demise as an independent company.

It is possible though unlikely that many of the issues that arose in this particular acquisition had been uncovered in the due diligence that the company did. Some certainly appear to those looking from afar to have been complete surprises to Quaker Oats.

ERM would not likely have been involved because it was neither well understood nor widely practiced at any level in 1994. Taking a look back on what did happen with this deal, it is hard to imagine that if ERM, when practiced competently within a risk-aware culture, would not have helped to avoid the risk trajectory of that acquisition. The table on the following page shows ERM in M&A.

Risk category	Actual situation	An ERM question	An ERM response
Competition	New competitors were arriving on the scene (e.g., Nantucket Nectars) and a major brand like PepsiCo was spending heavily on its Lipton brand iced tea. (PepsiCo bought Quaker Oats a few years later.)	Is there a risk that competition is heating up? How strong are the competitors?	Ask for analysis, if it shows competition is heating up. Plan mitigation. Shut down the deal, change the value of the acquisition pricing, or acquire one of the competitors too.
Marketing/ sales/ distribution	Former Snapple distributors did not want to sell lower-margin Gatorade from Quaker Oats as they were being asked to do and were unable to do business as usual. Snapple sales decreased after years of an upward trend.	Is there a risk that Snapple distributors will not want to do business the way we want them to—i.e., selling both Snapple and Gatorade?	Ask for surveys and/or interviews of distributors, if there might be issues. Plan mitigation. Retain separate distribution channels or revise distributor compensation or some other action.

Why Are M&As So Risk Laden?

All activity comes with risk. But not all activities come with the same level of risk. There are factors that make merging or acquiring companies significantly more risky than other activities. It is for this reason that ERM is so critically important in order to attain the objectives set for the merger or acquisition and to achieve long-term success from it. ERM offers the process and the know-how for identifying and planning mitigation for the risks associated with M&A.

Typical M&A risks include:

- Financials are not as represented and warranted by merger partner or acquired company; a weakened or unstable financial position is the actual case.

- Negative financial trend lines within the acquired entity accelerate exponentially just before or just after the deal is executed.

- Sales, in particular, have been inflated using any number of techniques by the merger partner or acquired company and are not as represented or warranted.

- Strained relationships with counterparties unbeknownst to the merger partner or acquiring company exist, which may affect planned objectives.

- Major litigation against the acquired company (pertaining to contract disputes, employment matters, compliance or regulatory issues, etc.) that is not yet initiated but imminent is not disclosed or found during due diligence.

- Major shareholder litigation over the M&A itself pertaining to deal specifics occurs, with deals over $100 million almost sure to attract such litigation.

- Regulators find an unexpected issue with the planned merger.

- Regulators delay the merger past planned merger date.

- Inventories are not as represented and warranted by the merger partner or acquired company, such that goods or materials are less than or more than stated or are not in a condition to be used or sold but have been hidden, camouflaged, or manipulated in some way.

- Intellectual property is not as represented or warranted by the merger partner or acquired company, whereby actual ownership is non-existent or in dispute.

- The acquirer has no expertise in the sector of the company being acquired and makes immediate mistakes in managing the acquired business.

- The acquirer has no experience in mergers and acquisitions and mismanages the change management effort needed to make the merger or acquisition successful (could be operational, cultural, or customer-facing issues).

- The acquirer expects to create synergies among things for which no synergies exist or can be made to exist.

- The acquirer overestimates efficiencies through economies of scale and/or underestimates the cost of accomplishing the efficiencies.

- Some factor that lessens the value of the acquired company, such as increasing competition, has been underestimated by the acquirer.

- The acquirer has miscalculated the tax consequences of the deal.

- The acquirer has failed to satisfy some regulatory filing and triggers a fine.

This is list is far from exhaustive. Most of the items in this short list could be powerful enough to negatively alter the outcome of an M&A in a significant way (or negatively affect a company as a whole).

The first point on the list was played out recently in story of Hewlett-Packard's purchase of Autonomy. On November 20, 2012, Matt Krantz reported "Hewlett-Packard, the struggling tech giant, stunned investors Tuesday, saying it will take an $8.8 billion write-down against earnings tied to alleged accounting improprieties at a company it bought last year."[2]

Consider some of the of the well-known M&As in recent history where the outcome was not what was expected or not positive: AOL/Time Warner, Daimler Benz/Chrysler, Citi/Travelers, Sears/Kmart, Bank of America/Countrywide, Quaker Oats/Snapple. There have been hundreds of lesser-known deals wherein the risks were not identified, or, if they were, they were not adequately managed.

The acquiring or merging company has to realize that only the tip of the iceberg is widely or easily known.

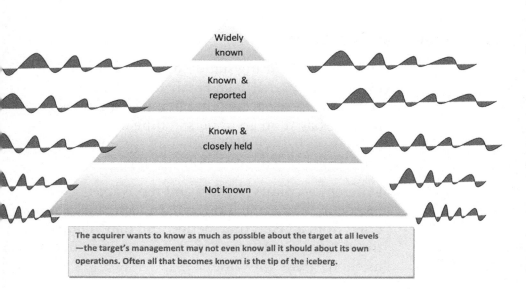

The acquirer wants to know as much as possible about the target at all levels —the target's management may not even know all it should about its own operations. Often all that becomes known is the tip of the iceberg.

None of this is to say that M&A is too risky to be done or that deals before the advent of ERM were not well managed. The point is that through practicing a robust form of ERM, companies can better ensure the success of a deal.

International M&A

If doing a deal within national borders can be uncertain, the uncertainty escalates with an international deal. A U.S. company might want to do a deal in another country for any of the reasons listed previously. One of the more recent chief reasons for U.S. companies doing an acquisition in Europe, for example, is to repatriate in the acquired company's county to take advantage of that country's lower corporate tax environment.

Whatever the reasons behind the deal, there are a great many added uncertainties around a cross-border deal. The quality of the due diligence becomes even more important in these cases, and with that quality comes more cost.

A short list of the risk elements would include the following:

Financial/Regulatory

- Different accounting standards may be in use. Even IAS's International Financial Reporting Standards (IFRS) means that financial analyses must be based on an understanding of the differences between U.S. generally accepted accounting practices (GAAP) and IFRS.

- Different accounts payable and receivable protocols may make it difficult to compare cash flows from a given time period and may hamper the ability to institute consistent or more efficient methods going forward.

- Additional and different regulatory bodies to deal with may create confusion and expose the acquirer to compliance breaches, however inadvertent.

- In some cases, countries require investments in their government bonds or other types of investments.

- Potential difficulties in repatriating profits from foreign operations.

Market

- Customer, vendor, and media reaction may not be what was expected either in the acquirer's country or in the target's country.

- Market trends may not have been understood as well or may not be as predictive as in the acquirer's country of origin.

Human resources

- The traditions and legal requirements surrounding issues of employment, termination, benefits, etc. are very different among countries, and these differences may be underestimated.

- The ability to move staff into the target's country may be more difficult than anticipated.

Risk: Deal or No Deal

It is easy to accept the premise that actually doing a merger or acquisition could expose the organization to unfavorable outcomes such as negative investor sentiment, share price decline, or margin or profit erosion, among others. It may be less easy to see how just announcing a potential deal could be almost as injurious as doing one that turns out bad.

Perhaps you have seen the drawing of a face that viewed from one direction appears to be a beautiful young woman but viewed from another direction appears to be an ugly old crone. When the news breaks about a projected deal, especially before all the reasoning and details concerning it are available, the market can react in unpredictable ways. Despite the fact that the party seeking the deal may be in fine financial or strategic shape and that good reasons exist for merging with or acquiring the target exist, appearances may be different.

For example, the reaction to a pharmaceutical company trying to buy another at what might be above fair value may create the impression that the acquiring company is in trouble or its new drug pipeline is dry and unpromising going forward. The reaction to an insurer trying to buy another with similar products and a similar geographic mix may create the impression that the company is unable to grow organically or has some other difficiency. If the deal fails to go through and the negative impression persists, a company could be hurt that would otherwise not be.

It behooves the deal maker to know that a perception risk exists and to take amelioration steps at the outset to truncate any negative spin that could occur—for example, by giving clear and convincing reasons for the deal that do not cite existing shortcomings.

Role of the Board

Each board of directors is unique in the way it plays its oversight role. Some boards are known to take a decidedly active role in mergers and acquisitions. Others tend to draw a line at the decision to do a deal or not.

Chinta Bhagat and Bill Huyett of McKinsey have a view on this that tracks with ours, namely that the independent and well-informed nature of board members means they can add perspective, advice, and know-how to a very uncertain undertaking.

> Many boards, reluctant to cross the line between governance and management, miss opportunities to help senior executives win at M&A. Boards are well placed to take a long-term view of a deal's value: the CEO or the business-unit leader may have tenures shorter than the time needed to realize it fully. Boards are also well positioned to challenge the biases that often cloud M&A decision making and goal setting. Furthermore, the diverse experiences of board members with long leadership careers in different corporate settings can shed useful light on common organizational risks in deals. Finally, boards can embolden senior management to pursue promising deals that may seem unfashionable or likely to be unpopular with investors initially.[3]

The Value of ERM Relative to M&A

Although a thorough and professional due diligence process is supposed to uncover the issues and uncertainties associated with a deal, ERM brings special risk identification skills and expertise to the due diligence exercise. In other words, it adds value to M&A in a number of ways:

- ERM ensures that the risks inherent to M&A for the specific company have been analyzed before looking at a specific deal. This avoids false starts or other premature actions that might misuse resources.

- ERM enhances all phases of due diligence and ensures that a risk perspective is brought to bear on all aspects of the data gathered during due diligence.

- ERM asks questions that would uncover both current and emerging risks to ensure transparency and well-informed decision making.

- ERM develops scenarios that allow the company to look at worst-case scenarios to test against its own risk tolerance.

- ERM minimizes surprises that might impact profitability, share price, and reputation.

- ERM provides the expertise for robust risk mitigation and contingency plans.

- ERM creates the narrative about risk to answer questions from external stakeholders.

Chapter 7

The Value of Applying ERM to New Marketing Ventures

New marketing ventures can take many forms. Chief among these are:

- Product expansion/new product launches
- Product enhancement launches
- New ad campaigns
- New ad spokespersons
- New sponsorships for marketing purposes
- Marketing events
- New/additional distribution channels
- Co-promotion and co-marketing partnering
- Target customer expansion
- Affinity marketing launches
- New/additional retail or Internet outlets
- Globalization

These activities are usually spelled out in the strategic plan and are aimed at increasing sales, bolstering brand awareness and relevancy, and/or diversifying the product line, customer segments, or geographies.

All of these take time and money to implement. In the case of new product launches, the R&D effort that precedes the launch will have required, in most cases, a significant outlay for the company. As such, a return on investment is very important, so it is important to address risks to its achievement.

ERM should play a part in all new marketing ventures to ensure that expected returns are met. Just as the company's strategy should be analyzed to ascertain the risks to strategic goals and objectives, the same type of analysis should be applied to an undertaking such as any one of these marketing ventures.

Bold Risk Taking in the Marketing Arena

Good marketing people know that when they introduce something new in the form of a product, advertising campaign, or distribution change there is risk involved. But are they able to see the risk objectively, evaluate its potential impact, and design effective risk monitoring and mitigation plans? Are they able to take these risk-related actions when they have so much to do just to implement the rollout of whatever innovation they are responsible for?

For example, in 2004 Tupperware started to sell its products in Target, a big box store. Up until then, its sales were through house parties its associates arranged, where the product could be discussed and the power of suggestion could encourage sales. Did Tupperware ever estimate how much revenue it could potentially lose from parties when it started to sell its products in Target stores, or did it only estimate how much revenue it might gain? Did it adjust for the risk in any way? Did it have a contingency plan if sales went poorly? What we do know is that The New York Times reported in its Business Section that "Tupperware Corporation will stop selling its plasticware in Target stores, saying the eight-month experiment hurt its core direct-sales business." [1]

In the pharmaceutical world, where joint marketing and joint development agreements are prevalent, a recent example involved Amgen's product Embrel, which was jointly marketed by Amgen's and Pfizer's sales forces. That agreement ended because Pfizer acquired a competing product, as the article in Medical Marketing & Media on-line edition states in its article's title "Enbrel reps risk layoff, as Pfizer calls early end to US selling"[2] Did this pose a risk for Amgen? For Pfizer? For the employees involved with the joint marketing endeavor?

The key question for our discussion about strategic partnerships is, do the parties to such agreements think through all the risks? In scenarios where one company contracts to have another company's sales force sell its product and the second company develops its own competing version of the product once the original is off patent, hasn't the first company given the second company an expertise advantage as it begins to sell its new product? And, if so, was this risk understood? Was it accounted for somewhere in the details and metrics of the original contract?

Bold marketing ideas and actions keep companies vital. At the same time, bold moves generally carry heavy risk. Such risk requires professional and thorough investigation and treatment. That is why the CRO and risk committee should be involved as they influence the application of the ERM process and principles to the marketing endeavor. This should result in ideas for finding the risks, ameliorating them, getting reimbursed for them, or planning contingencies for them.

The ERM Dynamic vis-à-vis Marketing

Identifying and addressing all or most of the risks that might apply to a particular marketing venture better ensure its success. The CRO should provide guidance on the risk identification methodology and organize surveys and other vehicles or forums that will elicit a comprehensive list of likely risks.

In practical terms, here are some of the ways that risk identification could be accomplished:

Ways to elicit risks	Who to involve
Survey instrument	Given to marketing department staff
Survey instrument	Given to ERM committee or senior team (C-suite)
Risk workshop/ brainstorming	Given to marketing department staff, possibly with other SMEs from different functions
Focus group	Made up of customers or distributors or random individuals
Brainstorming with independent and well-informed parties	Risk committee of the board

Once the risks have been identified via brainstorming, benchmarking, focus testing, and so on, then the process of quantifying and prioritizing begins. Ultimately, the highest-priority risks are addressed through action plans that are meant to eliminate, reduce, transfer, or accept the risk. For risks that are accepted and are high priority, the organization should have contingency or after-the-fact plans to address the impact should the risk actually materialize. These steps are basic and repeatable whenever risk management is applied to the strategy or to a function or to a business activity. There is an element of universality to the process.

No Ostriches Allowed

Marketing ventures are exciting. In planning one, there has to be a positive attitude about its chances for success. A problem arises when that attitude disallows a discussion of potential risks. It is too dangerous to let the idea generators, project planners, and management approvers put their heads in the sand like a flock of ostriches. Overcoming this very natural phenomenon is not easy. Simple approaches for working with those in charge of a major marketing effort are listed below.

- Rather than ask what the risks involved are, ask what absolutely needs to go as planned.

- Ask what risks competitors have experienced when they have undertaken something similar.

- Discuss upside and downside scenarios and what the cause of the downside ones could be.

- Ask for those involved to think of one risk they would like to avoid or have a mitigation or contingency plan for. Chances are, they will not be able to stop at just one risk.

Mitigate, Mitigate, Mitigate

Once risks are identified, quantified, and prioritized, the work of creating mitigation plans for the significant ones begins. Mitigation plans are aimed at individual risks and are unique based on myriad circumstances, such as the culture of the company, the amount of money that can be assigned, who is available to work on them, and so on.

Often with new marketing activities, there are winners and losers. For example, a distribution change may leave former distributors in the cold and disgruntled. A new product may mean that an old one has to be discontinued, and some customers may be unhappy that they can no longer obtain what they liked. A new advertising agency may mean that a previous one is retired from the account and may hold a grudge. These situations constitute a risk and should be mitigated. It is not enough to say that people forget their annoyance or anger. Some do forget. But others turn these feelings into dangerous acts of sabotage, reputation-damaging blogs, suits, or some other costly reaction. Of course, mitigation plans cannot wind up costing more than the risks themselves. Companies should also not succumb to any form of blackmail or bribery to avoid displeasing some group of stakeholders based on a legal and legitimate business decision.

Additionally, no mitigation plan is foolproof. So, some risk will always remain. Despite all these caveats, every effort should be made to mitigate against bad feelings by being honest, giving advance notice, offering alternatives if possible, and giving recompense if due to those who are negatively affected.

Mitigation tactics to address other categories of risk can include such things as:

- Pretesting in certain markets to mitigate risk up front

- Retaining some inventory of the discontinued or pre-enhanced product

- Being prepared with alternative advertising campaigns

- Having distributor or customer training materials at the ready in case they are needed

- Creating a series of contingency plans for various types of risks that might attach to the venture

- Executing contracts with sufficient cancellation "out" clauses and other protections

The Conundrum of Cross Sales

Any company that sells more than one product looks for ways to sell more of the company's products to the same customers, except in rare circumstances where the products are geared to entirely different customer groups or other special circumstances, such as prescription medicines. Cross-selling makes sense. It should increase total sales, increase efficiencies (one set of customer records, two sales to a known entity), and increase customer stickiness.

Notwithstanding all of the potential positives of cross-selling, there are some risks to be considered:

- If the second product purchased (possibly from a different business unit in the company) does not have the same quality as the first one that enabled the sale, could the customer be lost entirely?

- If the second product purchased (possibly from a different business unit in the company) is not serviced as well as the first one, could the customer be lost entirely?

- Could the second product somehow cannibalize the first one—in other words, so overtake the first one that the first one ceases to be purchased?

- Could issues among different business units about sales protocol, ownership of the customer, sales incentives, and/or record keeping become so disabling that the benefit of the cross sale is cancelled?

In looking at the risks of cross-selling, one enters the world of unintended consequences. It is a state where what should be positive becomes negative because of some condition that exists that should not exist, or some condition is given rise to even though it was not wished for or expected.

Once again, ERM can help to identify many of these unintended consequences well in advance of their materializing and can help to create techniques for mitigating or eliminating them by imposing the rigor of a process aimed at identifying, quantifying and addressing risk.

A similar set of risks can be generated from adding new distribution channels or any other major change to marketing, sales, and/or branding of a company or its products.

The Value of ERM Relative to Marketing Ventures

Some of the benefits of applying ERM to marketing have been alluded to in the preceding paragraphs. One of the most important is the impartiality of professionals outside the marketing function. Through this objectivity ERM will provide these beneficial outcomes:

- A carefully compiled list of risks that have the potential to be eliminated or minimized—only by knowing the risks can an organization defend against them

- Well-developed best- and worst-case scenarios that can help to create more realistic outcomes and objectives for the venture, which increases the chance for success

- Enhanced control over unintended consequences—by thinking through how the venture will be perceived by all stakeholders, it is less likely that the venture will result in something antithetical to what was intended

- Fewer surprises for the organization—marketing, manufacturing, distribution, etc.

All of the above outcomes contribute to increased revenues, reduced waste, and greater profitability.

Chapter 8

The Value of Applying ERM to Talent Management

Talent Management/Human Resources and Risk

Talent management is a crucial and timely issue for business for many reasons, including:

- An aging workforce can leave significant expertise gaps as baby boomers retire.

- Technological advances change the nature of the skills and knowledge that is required by the workforce.

- More recent generations have diverse wants, needs, and approaches to their careers, which creates complexity in attracting, motivating, and retaining needed talent.

- Technological advances change the nature of the skills and knowledge that are required by the workforce.

- The ability of organizations to afford the type of benefit plans (retirement, medical, relocation) that were previously customary has been lost due to the cost of such plans, and this stresses the relationship between the organization and its talent.

- Increased legislation and regulation make ethical and legal compliance vital, so monitoring and managing the behavior of the individuals in the talent pool becomes even more critical.

These issues create risk. There is a risk that organizations may not be able to locate or develop talent fast enough to fill positions that retirees are leaving or that new technology demands. There is the risk that organizations will experience high turnover and take longer to fill open positions because there is not a match between what they need and what potential applicants are looking for—for example, time off, no relocations, job rotations. There is a risk that benefit plans will increase costs to breaking points. There is the risk that without the binding power of defined benefit retirement plans or reduced-cost medical plans loyalty will disappear, turnover will escalate, and the impetus to do a good job will erode. There is a risk that workers, at any level, will inadvertently or purposefully expose the organization to compliance breaches or other dangerous unethical or fraudulent events. Indeed, the HR function manages a variety of programs and processes that carry risk. All of these risks can benefit from an ERM approach.

When People Are the Risk

In addition to these systemic issues that create risk, there is also the very basic risk that an individual can do something bad or wrong with huge consequences.

A stunning example of this involves the former Barings Bank in the United Kingdom.

> The most famous "rogue trader" in history, Nick Leeson, brought down one of the grandest names in British banking.
>
> Working in Barings' Singapore office, Leeson initially made large profits for the bank by dealing in derivatives and futures. But after running up losses, he hid his bad trades in a single account in 1992.
>
> These losses grew over several years, forcing him into a series of increasingly desperate but unsuccessful attempts to make the money back. Leeson finally fled in February 1995 after a bet that the Tokyo stock market would rise went badly wrong.
>
> Once the full scale of the losses became apparent, Barings was sold to Dutch bank ING for just £1.[1]

What could be a better example to represent this phenomenon? Does ERM eliminate this risk? No. Does ERM identify the individual who should be watched more closely because they pose the risk? No. What does ERM do?

Staying with this particular example, through the ERM process, the following could and should be done:

- Identify the risk that rogue trades might occur.

- Identify the most likely areas within the trading environment where it might occur.

- Report the risk as part of the normal ERM process.

- Work with internal audit, compliance, and other appropriate areas to mitigate the risk

- Ensure there is a containment, contingency, and communication plan in place should the risk materialize.

- Include the risk as part of risk appetite and risk tolerance discussions.

These actions better enable an organization to avoid or withstand this type of individual act.

Talent and Litigation

People are a risk in another way, too. Your employee or an applicant for an open position can be a source of expensive litigation. This can be the case whether or not there is justification for the suit. A recent study by Hiscox Insurance gives statistics that provide a clear picture of how pervasive the risk of being sued by employees is:

A new study of employment practices litigation (EPL) data by Hiscox, the international specialist insurer, found four states—California, Illinois, Alabama and Mississippi—along with the District of Columbia, to be the top five riskiest areas of the US for employee lawsuits. Businesses in these states and jurisdictions face a substantially higher risk of being sued by their employees compared to the national average.

According to the study, on average, a US-based business with at least 10 employees has a 12.5% chance of having an employment liability charge filed against them. However, businesses in several states face a much higher level of exposure to litigation. California has the most frequent incidences of EPL charges in the country, with a 42% higher chance of being sued by an employee for establishments with at least 10 employees over the national average. Other states and jurisdictions where employers are at a high risk of employee suits include the District of Columbia (32% above the national average), Illinois (26%), Alabama (25%), Mississippi (19%), Arizona (19%) and Georgia (18%). Lower-risk states for EPL charges include West Virginia, Massachusetts, Michigan, Kentucky and Washington.[2]

At the national level, the EEOC requested a $12 million increase to its budget and has firmed up its goals. Here is an excerpt from its congressional budget justification:

Outcome Goal II.A
Members of the public understand and know how to exercise their right to employment free of discrimination.

Outcome Goal II.B
Employers, unions and employment agencies (covered entities) prevent discrimination and better resolve EEO issues, thereby creating more inclusive workplaces.

Strategy II.A.1: Target outreach to vulnerable workers and underserved communities.

Strategy II.B.1: Target outreach to small and new businesses.[3]

The awareness that ERM creates about this risk area may make the difference between the development and enforcement of proper employment practices and policies versus a more laid-back approach that results in inappropriate, unethical, or illegal actions. Another way of saying this is that ERM is often the catalyst for recognizing the significance of people-related risks. Recognition leads to greater compliance and standards of care that will protect against employment complaints and suits.

Unengaged, Zoned Out, but Employed

Throughout history, there have always been employees who have not loved the work they do. The work may have been backbreaking, monotonous, or underpaid. Working conditions may have been dangerous, uncomfortable, or uninviting. As technology has made work easier in many ways and working conditions have been made more comfortable or even ergonomic and stylish, employees have not necessarily become more enamored of their jobs.

In fact, a recent Gallup survey found that "The bulk of employees worldwide—63%—are 'not engaged,' meaning they lack motivation and are less likely to invest discretionary effort in organizational goals or outcomes. And 24% are 'actively disengaged,' indicating they are unhappy and unproductive at work and liable to spread negativity to coworkers. In rough numbers, this translates into 900 million not engaged and 340 million actively disengaged workers around the globe."[4]

This is not good news for any employer for many reasons, but chief among them is the fact that unengaged workers create risk. They may be more prone to producing poor-quality products (product recall risk), having accidents (workers compensation and absenteeism risk), turning to unethical behavior (reputational and fine/fee/closure risk), and so on.

Add to this the results of other studies that show there are significant numbers of employees coming to the workplace under the influence of drugs or alcohol and the picture becomes even more ominous. Employees under the influence may pose huge threats in terms of accidents to themselves and others and to property, as well as exhibit erratic and dangerous behavior.

Employees need to be managed. Why else would there be a need for organizational hierarchies, performance review processes, and other human resource policies and procedures? Yet, the real risks inherent in the workforce have often been underestimated, forgotten, or consciously overlooked. ERM can be the antidote to insufficient attention to this risk area simply by focusing on the subject of risk in this arena.

Keeping the Focus on Talent-Related Risks

It is not altogether uncommon for organizations to laser focus on certain aspects of the business or business activities when it comes to the risk inherent in them but to cast only a glancing eye on other aspects or activities. It is less likely that this uneven view will occur when an ERM process is in place. This is especially true because once a risk is quantified, it is more difficult to relegate it as a second-tier risk if it has the same potential impact of something that has always been seen as a first-tier risk.

People and people-related risks can sometimes be elevated to a first-tier risk and still be ignored.

A good example of this phenomenon is trend line for wage and hour suits brought under the Fair Labor Standards Act and enforced by the Department of Labor. The following report sets out some of the details. Wage and hour lawsuits have reached a surprise record high, according to a report by law firm Seyfarth Shaw LLP.

Cases filed under the Fair Labor Standards Act (FLSA) have continued to skyrocket in 2013, despite indications that these filings had moderated during the past 12 months, the firm said.

There were 7,764 FLSA cases filed in 2013, up 10 percent from 2012 which saw 7,064 cases filed, according to data from the Federal Judicial Center.

Richard Alfred, chair of Seyfarth's wage and hour litigation practice, said the claims forming the bulk of these numbers include misclassification of employees, alleged uncompensated "work" performed off the clock and miscalculation of overtime pay for non-exempt workers.[5]

This trend of skyrocketing filings could have been predicted by looking at just a couple of very big settlements in the mid 2000s, such as Allstate's $120 million dollar settlement in 2006 concerning overtime pay.[6] Another was Wal-Mart's $54 million dollar settlement in 2008 over wages concerning break times that were not permitted.[7]

Companies should have started to ensure compliance to the FLSA as a result of these high-profile cases, which served to encourage employees of many other companies to follow suit and redress their grievances. Instead, company after company chose to ignore the risk. Some did it because they thought they were saving money; others did it because it made things easier administratively. In the end, many companies created nightmares for themselves because they did not take the risk seriously.

In an effort to get employers to take wage and hour regulations more seriously, the Maryland Court of Appeals on August 13, 2014, held for the employee in Peters v. Early Healthcare Giver, Inc. and allowed for treble damages.[8] It would be expected that a company practicing ERM, such regulations would be taken more seriously and risks associated with breaching regulations would be identified and addressed.

As more undocumented workers find their way into the country and local governments look for ways to increase revenue, the next wave of fines and/or litigation in the employment arena may involve undocumented workers. Hefty fines have been levied by Immigration and Customs Enforcement already. It will be important for companies to examine the risk that they may be making hiring decisions without sufficient knowledge or governance in order to comply with national, state, and local regulations.

Another situation that involves risk for many companies is adequate pension funding. Although the underfunding situation greatly improved by the end of 2013 due to better market conditions, billions of dollars of underfunding still exists in both the public and the private spheres. During the depths of the underfunding, many organizations chose to put this people or human resource risk on the sidelines while hoping for improved investment returns or some sort of miracle—although some organizations did take the action of addressing the future risk of pension underfunding by eliminating their defined benefit plans for new employees in favor of defined contribution plans as they paid out lump sums to vested employees.

The risks inherent in an underfunded pension situation are just as much about solvency and compliance as they are about the ability (or inability) to retain talent and the difficulty in recruiting new talent as the health of the company's pension funding becomes well known.

Because overfunding, on the other hand, is not optimal for an organization, achieving the right balance between under and overfunding is a goal. There is risk inherent tipping the pendulum too far one way or another. Pension funding would be expected to be a risk that an ERM managed company would examine carefully and deal with appropriately.

A fundamental talent-related risk is the lack of enlightened leadership. Think of all the people you know who have left a job. How often is it because of the boss? Even if the poor leadership does not result in the subordinate's leaving, it can result in all sorts of destructive behavior.

Leadership is an art that requires special talents. Absent those talents, it takes excellent management in an organization to overcome the risks of high turnover, unrealized potential, and even counter-productivity among its talent. In today's war for talent, these are profound risks.

Working from the Castle

With the massive shift of work from offices to homes comes a dramatically different set of risks for organizations that have made such a shift.

The uncertainties surrounding this new work environment include:

- Will there be adequate supervision to ensure the quality of work?

- Will there be adequate supervision to ensure work is performed in the time frame that is prescribed for the position?

- Will workers compensation insurance respond if there is an accident or injury given that the employer has so limited control over ergonomics and safety?

- How is or can data security be assured in the off-site setting?

- How is or can other work products or equipment be secured in the off-site setting?

- How does this arrangement affect the employee's ability to be integrated into an office environment when necessary?

These and other uncertainties add to the human resources risk picture for an organization. ERM will highlight the most significant of these risks, especially any unique ones that may exist for a particular organization.

Keeping the Talent Pool Filled

Organizations cannot operate without people, whether the entity is a single-owner proprietorship or a company with fifty thousand employees. People power the organization.

Raw power alone, however, is not enough. For the organization to succeed it needs not just power but skilled power. Take away the necessary skills and failure will follow.

There is much talk about the fact that the U.S. workforce is aging and a lot of experienced and skilled labor will be exiting. One could look at this as the normal cycle of one group of talent leaving the door open for the next group to take its place. The risk revolves around the uncertainty of whether or not the next group is sufficient in number, experience, and behavior to fill the gap left by those retiring.

According to a report published in 2013 by the Society for Human Resource Management, 73% of respondents said that a shortage of skilled workers will have a major impact on the U.S. workplace in the next five years.[9]

This risk will impact some industries or areas of the country more than others. Still, it is a major overall area of risk. It is one that will require careful strategic and mitigation action planning to address.

The Value of ERM Relative to Talent Management

A major benefit of ERM is its ability to put the spotlight on talent-related risks, which are so often overlooked. By doing so, these risks can be given the attention they need.

By recognizing these risks and taking action, it is much more possible to:

- Avoid or limit the potential damage from rogue employees.
- Attract and retain talent.
- Eliminate talent voids.
- Minimize employment-related complaints or suits.

- Avoid or limit fees, fines, or penalties from being out of compliance with laws and regulations.

- Lessen people-related surprises.

- Enhance reputation.

Chapter 9

The Value of Applying ERM to Change Management

Change is inevitable. Organizations change in both formal and informal ways. Given the amount of risk that change creates, organizations need to manage change-related risk deliberately and comprehensively.

Formal Change Management Initiatives

There are many types of change management initiatives that require formal project management approaches. Most common among these are:

- Major technology initiatives to improve business processes based on customer expectations and competitive pressures or the need to be more efficient and cost-effective

- Enterprise-wide expense-saving initiatives to cut costs, which may include changes to processes, technology, vendor guidelines, workloads, staffing levels, outsourcing, reimbursement policies, compensation, or any number of other areas

- Large-scale organizational design initiatives to reduce layers of management, speed decision making, and/or take advantage of better locales for doing business

- Cultural initiatives to create a new culture within the staff, typically focused on creating a more results-oriented or a more customer-centric culture

Risks to Change

As so many quotes and sayings about change suggest, change is not often welcome, nor is it easy. By its very nature, change involves uncertainty. In other words, there is significant risk involved with change initiatives, and the scales tip in favor of negative, not positive, risk. This means that the odds of failure are higher than those of success.

In fact, in 1995, John Kotter published research that revealed that only 30% of change programs are successful.[1] Fast-forward to 2008. A recent McKinsey and Company survey of business executives indicates that the percentage of change programs that are a success today is still 30%. "The field of 'change management,' it would seem, hasn't changed a thing."[2]

Failure can take many shapes. Here are some of them:

- The change never materializes, and the project fails to produce a result.

- The product of the change does not turn out to be what was planned or does not perform as planned.

- Some product of the change does come about as planned but is not accepted or adopted by staff or customers as planned.

- The product of the change does come about as planned but at a cost so above budget that it causes severe financial damage.

- The product of the change does come about as planned but too late to be of any good.

Among the most prevalent proximate causes of these failures are:

- The desired outcome is too difficult to achieve in the present circumstances—in other words, it was overpromised and underdelivered. Perhaps it was the CEO's vision or the CIO's bid to become center of attention.

- Resistance to the particular change is more powerful than the forces of change.

- Other priorities legitimately or illegitimately rob the change project of its necessary resources, such as talent, time, or money. Often the time it takes to make change happen is underestimated, or it is unjustifiably reasoned that change must be implemented quickly because momentum cannot be sustained.

- Lack of cooperation purposefully or inadvertently caused the project to fail.

ERM in the Picture

How does ERM fit into the picture? Before answering that question, it should be noted that most change management or project management processes have an element of risk identification and contingency planning embedded within them. As good as this might be, a major change needs to managed and viewed within the bigger picture, just as a business unit is managed both within itself and also within the larger corporate entity. Anything that separates the effort from mainstream processes and systems, anything that isolates it too fully from the attention, resources, and momentum of the organization as whole, could diminish its chance of success. If ERM has as its goal finding and treating all risks to the strategy of the organization, then it must find and treat the risks to any major change effort the organization has undertaken.

It is up to the key players at both the corporate ERM and change management project levels to determine how to work together to make risk identification, mitigation, and reporting as seamless and lacking in duplication as possible. This can take the form of having an ERM practitioner be part of the change project team, for example. By doing so, the risk identification techniques that an experienced ERM practitioner brings can be applied in real time within the scope of the change effort.

Some Mitigation Tactics

Because many risks to a successful change effort are fairly well known, having been experienced by so many companies involved in so many change initiatives, it is possible for seasoned risk and change specialists to quickly summon a number of mitigation tactics that can be used when necessary.

Risk	Tactic
Lack of support for the change	Create the imperative for change—for example, the change is not about lowering expenses, but about not letting the competition get an upper hand and hurting your business.
Lack of CEO or senior leadership	Ensure that the CEO and senior leaders are invested in the change effort via their compensation and use technology to have them send messages and stay informed of progress.
Inability of staff to take on change, adapt, and do more than their "day jobs"	Prepare staff for the initiative rather than just announcing it. Adjust workloads or add temporary staff. Bring in special expertise, if necessary.
Negative unintended consequences occur with external stakeholders, such as customers or distributors	Take periodic stock of how the changes are affecting and being received by external stakeholders to avoid having customers or distributors jump ship.
Actual costs exceed projected costs and change effort goes over budget	Build reserve into the initiative's budget. Have a contingency list of alternative ways to deal with cost overruns—e.g., "nice to haves" that can be deleted from project specifications or leverage points to use in negotiating costs with the vendors and consultants employed in project.

Every organization will need to determine the distinct risks it faces in the wake of change initiatives and then determine the mitigation tactics that might be employed against the risk. In the case of change projects, the identification of risks will likely need to be done more frequently than in the case of more stable conditions. This will allow for tactics to be put in place in a timely fashion before risk takes the initiative too far off track.

Such a periodic risk review can and should be built into the overall project plan.

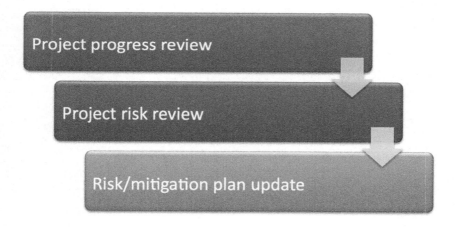

Project progress review

Project risk review

Risk/mitigation plan update

The Value of ERM Relative to Change Management

ERM informs the change management initiative of real and serious risks to the successful completion of the project's objectives. It provides the framework for identifying, prioritizing, mitigating, and monitoring the risks.

One of the unique advantages that can be gained from an ERM approach to change initiatives is that risks are not sublimated and left to develop unabated. Given the importance of and management's demand for staff support and enthusiasm for a change initiative, it is very common for staff to be afraid to voice concerns or risks. The fear stems from the possibility that an earnest attempt to alert the organization to a risk might be seen as lack of support, reluctance to change, inability to learn new skills, or just plain whining. An ERM culture allows for real risks to be legitimately voiced. Thus, the initiatives' chance of ultimate success is increased because surprises are minimized and risks are mitigated. This saves the organization expense and time and protects morale and reputation.

Chapter 10

The Value of Applying ERM to Finance

Finance professionals know a lot about risk and can do complex risk/reward calculations, whether applied to investment portfolios, credit arrangements, budgets and capital expenditures, or other financial activities. The question is whether these professionals have the ability to look at risk from the broadest perspective possible as they make recommendations or take action on the myriad areas in their remit. These areas include investments, lines of credit, debt levels, debt vehicles, credit terms, payables terms, budgets, financial reporting, and so on.

A Major Way ERM Helps Finance

In an ERM environment, the finance team gains insights from the ERM (risk) committee or from risk surveying done throughout the organization or from research sponsored by the CRO or ERM leader.

- Are things happening within the company's customer segments that might affect creditworthiness that only the marketing team might be aware of? Does what is happening present a heightened credit risk? Would finance recommend modification to credit terms, if it knew?

- Are questions or issues being discussed among investors that the investor relations team may be picking up? Is there a risk that investors without sufficient information or explanation regarding these issues may have misguided negative reactions to the company? Would finance do something differently in regard to financial reporting if it knew of these issues?

- Are pension and benefits regulatory changes looming that may affect expenses that HR has the best understanding of? Is there a risk that budgets will be understated? Would finance do something differently in terms of budget preparations and communications or pension funding if it knew of these potential changes at the earliest possible time?

- Are there risks to the achievement of revenue targets that no one is talking about? What would finance do differently if it knew this likelihood and significance of the risks relative to budget guidelines, credit lines, or messaging to the capital markets?

As hypothetical as these questions may be, they illustrate how important it is for risk information to cross functional boundaries. ERM fosters a culture where risk is always being considered and where it is transparent and discussed so that it can be avoided or mitigated.

Innovation Risk

The general public tends to think of innovation in terms of new technology, pioneering medical procedures and drugs, and novel fashions in clothing and home furnishings. But the world of finance has not lacked in innovation, either. Consider the following:

- Credit default swaps
- ETFs
- Insurance-linked securities
- Derivatives of derivatives
- Exotic hedges
- New currencies—for example, Bitcoin

These innovations carry risk, as most financial vehicles do. However, some carry heightened risk. The more complex, untested, and/or unregulated the instrument, the more risk it carries.

In addition to the above innovations, there is a plethora of new or previously obscure trading practices such as high-speed trading, secondary exchanges, dark pools (private exchanges or forums for trading securities), and after-hours trading. These may take away risk for some investors, such as big traders, but increase risk for others, such as retail investors.

In an effectively managed ERM process, there would be discussion and analysis around the risks associated with new vehicles and levels of accumulation in them. These discussions and analyses would result in the company's taking the appropriate actions in terms of limiting, hedging, mitigating, and contingency planning to guard against the associated risks.

This is not to say that innovative financial instruments are too risky to trade in or use; it is just to say that they need to be approached in a risk-aware manner. After the financial crisis of 2008 the then U.S. secretary of the treasury, Timothy Geithner, was quoted as saying, "it has become clear since the implosion of AIG . . . last September that numerous players in these markets failed to understand the risks they were taking on."[1]

The Return Tug of War

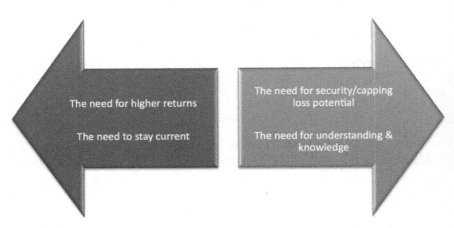

The need for higher returns

The need to stay current

The need for security/capping loss potential

The need for understanding & knowledge

That subprime loans existed and were widely used was known before 2008 by bankers, institutional investors and rating agencies. It was also known that home values were at heights that awed most homeowners and homebuyers. So, knowledge of the primary vehicle in that aspect of the 2008 crisis was not an issue. The issue involved some of the investment vehicles that were derived from subprime lending, the accumulations that certain institutions took in these vehicles, and an overall lack of connecting the dots among high home values, escalating mortgage rates, subprime borrowers, and stagnating wages that allowed those vehicles to be rated as safer than they actually were.

Shifting Sands

Very fertile sources of risk for finance are changes to accounting standards and the gray areas that have yet to be clarified. In the first seven months of 2014 there were already fourteen updates to the generally accepted accounting principles (GAAP) issued by the Financial Accounting

Standards Board (FASB). On top of whatever goes on within U.S. GAAP is the continuing debate about the United States' potential adoption of the International Financial Reporting Standards (IFRS) in place of GAAP.

Many U.S. companies have already adopted IFRS because of their own globalization. Consider the number of companies that have operations or sales offices abroad, the many companies that have international shareholders, and those that are now doing M&As abroad for improved tax treatment or other reasons. IFRS makes sense for these companies, even without it being mandatory. Other companies are running parallel reports while they consider a changeover. If IFRS does replace GAAP in the United States at some point in the future, it will be a massive effort involving everything from school curricula to the code in automated systems within accounting firms and corporations.

Risk related to these many accounting changes takes the form of accounting errors and possible restatements, potential interpretation issues on the part of analysts and investors, and strain on staff time and abilities.

ERM can help the finance function think through what the risks may be and how they might be addressed. ERM can also assist by making sure the rest of the functions and business units in the company understand the significant effort and risks involved in the transition.

Risk in Many Forms

ERM can neither eliminate all risks nor prevent certain risks from emerging, but it can and does nurture a culture that is ever conscious of the presence of risk. It makes the discussion of risk part of strategizing and decision making. Very importantly, it creates the ability for employees to cite a risk to the achievement of some objective without looking like or being labeled a naysayer or a sandbagger.

In an interview for an article published in May 2014 about risk management issues, challenges, and tips, Gary Alterson, senior director for risk and advisory services for Neohapsis, defined the biggest challenge in this way: "A lack of an open, risk-aware culture. In order to build a culture where business managers are willing to be transparent to their executives, the executives have to be careful to craft the kind of culture that fosters this transparency. Open dialogs about concerns, risks, and trade-offs necessary without 'shooting the messenger' are often missing in organizations that lack effective risk management."[2]

As part of fostering risk awareness, ERM supports the finance team when making a financial decision in a gray area. By considering the risks associated with various decision scenarios, many issues, costs, and negative unintended consequences can be avoided.

ERM can bring value to the finance function; the finance function can bring value to ERM. In particular, the CFO and financial team will likely have a role to play in ERM when it comes to setting the risk appetite and risk tolerance of the company.

Risk appetite
How willing is the company to accept risk to profits, revenue, or reputation in general terms: somewhat, not at all, or very much?

Risk tolerance
How willing is the company to accept risk to profits, revenue, or reputation in specific terms—e.g., a 10% variance on revenues, a 5% variance on profits, or no tolerance relative to reputation?

The ERM process brings the need for setting these parameters to the forefront. In most companies, the finance team would run a number of financial scenarios and develop a recommended appetite and tolerance level. This recommendation would then be presented to the C-Suite and to the board for final approval. Next, these positions and thresholds would be communicated to the rest of the organization.

As part of the overall ERM process, the impact levels assigned to prioritized risks would be cross-referenced against the tolerance levels to help determine how much mitigation needs to be applied to the risk. For example, if a single risk had a potential impact that would reach 80% of the company's tolerance, that risk might get most of the mitigation attention or budget or cause a change to strategy. Likewise, if the impact of a certain three risks equaled 90% of the tolerance, they would get special attention.

Thus, although the risks themselves may still exist, the risk of exceeding these well-thought-out thresholds is greatly diminished. When living with and within these thresholds becomes a well-established pattern of corporate behavior, it should translate into reduced volatility in many spheres, such as earnings, share price, cost of insurance, and other fluctuations.

In fact, a great example of the relationship between ERM and reduced volatility comes from work done by Aon PLC in close collaboration with the Wharton School of the University of Pennsylvania. A November 2013 report stated: "Working with the annual financial results for an increased sample of 361 publicly traded companies and using Bloomberg market data from March 2011 to March 2013, researchers at Aon and Wharton continue to evidence a statistical link between high levels of risk maturity and higher relative stock price returns along with lower levels of relative stock price volatility."[3]

The Value of ERM Relative to Finance

The value that ERM bring to financial activities and responsibilities is manifold. From providing multiple perspectives on risk to initiating discussions about risk tolerance, ERM can help finance manage risks and enable it to help the organization to manage risks.

Chapter 11

The Value of ERM to the Supply Chain and Sourcing

It is obvious that regardless of industry, properly managing the supply chain is critical to success in most organizations.

Supply chain management (SCM) aims to streamline and maintain the procurement process by involving various stakeholders involved with procurement across the enterprise. This includes five basic elements of the procurement process: (1) planning, (2) sourcing, (3) making and buying, (4) distributing, and (5) the dispersal of goods and services necessary for the organization to operate properly.

Because SCM is an enterprise-based process, it mirrors the breadth of enterprise risk management. There is inherent risk within supply chain operations, thus SCM and ERM intersect. Risk identification and mitigation within any ERM approach to SCM will span many business functions, including logistics, finance, operations, and HR. A well-designed SCM process will need to work hand in hand with a well-designed ERM process in order to ensure uninterrupted supply flow and ultimately the successful achievement of critical business strategies and objectives.

Identifying the Value of ERM in Supply Chain Management

As we have discussed previously in this book and in ***Enterprise Risk Management: Straight to the Point***, the focus of any sound ERM process needs to start with the corporate strategy. The same can be said for SCM. Every part of well-designed SCM should be in support of ensuring strategic success. By applying ERM techniques to the SCM process, SCM is in a stronger position to achieve its contribution to the overall strategy. Likewise, to be successful, ERM needs to span all aspects of the enterprise. By integrating ERM into the SCM process, the success of both is better ensured.

Much of what has been written on the subject of ERM tends to be academic in nature and often leans toward the theoretical. Although commendable, a theoretical approach to ERM does not win the confidence of senior management or others who demand that the value of a process needs to be measured and identified in clear terms of bottom-line benefits. The intersection of SCM and ERM can achieve measurable results.

SCM is generally subject to rigorous measurements. It uses many highly quantitative concepts, such as just-in-time inventory and lean manufacturing, as well as other highly measureable management techniques. Since it deals with what is measurable, supply chain risk can also be measured. As discussed in chapter 4, if the risk can be measured, then the value of managing that risk can also be measured. Thus, the value of ERM as related to SCM can clearly be demonstrated.

The supply chain process can involve many business operations, including offshore manufacturing, outsourcing activities, global sourcing, and other highly coordinated and interdependent processes. Each of these has clearly identifiable inherent risks that should be identified and understood. These may take the form of risks to the brand or reputation, information technology breaches, or logistical failures. Supply chain disruptions due to unexpected and undesirable geopolitical events, regulatory changes, or even man-made or natural disasters are quite common. Each of these potential risks must be identified and understood to appropriately transfer or mitigate each of them.

A Case for Categorization

A recent survey by MIT and Pricewaterhouse Coopers (PWC) list a number of sources of supply chain risk (SCR).[1]

Interestingly, but not surprisingly, the sources they list are quite similar to the risk categories we described in *Enterprise Risk Management: Straight to the Point*:

Financial	**Legal and regulatory**
Geopolitical	**Industry/marketplace**
Strategic	**Catastrophic**
Human resources	**Operational**
Environmental	**Contracts and Third Party Relationships**
Information technology	**Reputational**

Key risks identified in the MIT study fit nicely into a number of these categories.

- Raw material price fluctuation and currency flux (financial risk)

125

- Market changes and energy prices (industry/marketplace risk)

- Environmental catastrophes and raw material scarcity (environmental risk)

- Rising labor costs (human resources risk)

- Geopolitical instability (geopolitical risk)

- Partner/supplier instability (customer/Third Party Relationship contracting risk)

- Changing technology, IT disruptions, outages, cyber attacks (information technology risk)

By establishing a clear set of categories for risk identification, key elements of the business plan can be easily mapped to various SCRs. So, in many respects, each of these two functions then should easily contribute to the other.

The ERM process is then positioned to bring value to the SCM process by clearly identifying SCRs that will directly affect the success of the business plan.

In order to clearly identify all significant risks, the PWC survey principals suggest the establishment of a supply chain risk leadership council (SCRLC) and a supply chain risk management (SCRM) team. They describe an effective SCRM team as including leaders from functions such as business continuity, engineering and design, finance, import/export compliance, logistics, manufacturing, procurement, quality, security, and supplier management.

In *Enterprise Risk Management: Straight to the Point*, we described the establishment of a risk committee. If appropriately designed, the risk committee established for the overall ERM process should be composed of a membership quite similar to that described by the SCRLC. The value of ERM as it relates to SCM then is that it may eliminate any duplicative efforts of a separate SCRM team.

A Governance Aspect of ERM Value as Applied to SCM

As we will describe in chapter 12, a key value of ERM is that if properly designed, the ERM program is carried down throughout the organization from the highest level of decision makers to those who are on the front lines of operations making day-to-day tactical supply chain decisions. The more risk-aware these frontline managers are, the more effective they will be in dealing with risk as it relates to the supply chain process. Thus ERM brings a value to both the supply chain and governance objects at the same time.

Just as ERM may contribute significantly to the SCM process, the SCM process may contribute to the overall ERM process.[2] SCM is likely one of the more mature processes within a corporation. A well-established SCM process will have a number of metrics, such as operational performance, and financial benefits that are designed to determine value of SCM to the organization. These same metrics may contribute to measuring the value of ERM. In addition, a mature SCM provides a number of process benefits that lend themselves directly to the overall ERM process. These include:

- Process consistency, which serves to reduce redundant efforts

- Improved communication

- Improved ability to anticipate potential risks and perhaps time to develop effective mitigation plans

- A means to measure risk across the enterprise

- The identification of risk that might not have been recognized by other means

So, in general, the SCM and ERM processes should be closely tied and aligned to bring the greatest value to the organization.

As ERM and SCM need to be closely aligned, it is worth viewing how ERM contributes value to the five key elements of supply chain management.[3]

1. Planning

2. Choosing suppliers

3. Manufacturing

4. Delivery or logistics

5. Defect and excess

Each of these elements comes with its own set of inherent risks.

The first stage of most SCM processes is simply planning. Executives and managers develop strategies to manage resources for manufacturing operations and efficient product delivery. Metrics are developed to monitor progress and compliance.

One of the key benefits of a well-established ERM process is how much it can contribute to the business planning process. One essential element of an ERM program is the development of a risk catalog or risk inventory, a list of all the risks that have been previously identified as they may relate to a given business strategy. It is a permanent record of situations or events that may have an effect on the successful outcome of a strategy or goal. During the planning phase of SCM, these risks or risk factors, having already been identified, can simplify the process of identifying risk related to the supply chain. Essentially, by relying on work that has already been accomplished via ERM, the SCM process can be streamlined.

Choosing your suppliers is the second step. One of the categories that should always be considered when evaluating risks related to strategy are third-party contracts. This should include contracts with customers, third-party service providers, and, of course, suppliers. The collective risk identified during this process should provide valuable input into choosing new suppliers or reviewing existing suppliers. In choosing suppliers, it would be best not to choose a supplier that, while satisfactory for supply chain needs, could have an impact on other strategic areas. For example, a division or subsidiary of the company may have experienced shipment delays or quality issues that affected its ability to achieve a corporate objective not specifically related to a normal supply chain–dependent division. By reviewing the risk catalog, as mentioned in the previous step, this risk may have been identified and the issue could be mitigated before any new risk event with the particular supplier occurred. It enables the company to take a truly enterprise view of risk.

The manufacturing phase is perhaps the most critical element. It is here that the benefits of sound ERM processes employed during the planning and supplier selection phases will bear fruit and lessen many of the risk inherent within manufacturing of goods.

During the manufacturing process, a sound ERM process should ensure that strong project risk management processes are in place. Consideration of six sigma or other quality management process should be in place to reduce manufacturing risk while also providing valuable feed back to the other enterprise plans that are being viewed under ERM.

Delivery, or logistics, is the fourth stage of SCM. There are many risks to consider in this step, many of which might have already been identified or addressed by the ERM program. Risk categories that could directly affect delivery or logistics could include technology risks. One key technology risk could be in global location number (GLN) implementation. GLN is a good example of an enterprise-level system risk that could affect all of the company's suppliers. GLN is a system based on thirteen-digit numbers developed by GS1, a neutral, international not-for-profit organization that is used to identify parties and physical locations. The locations identified with GLN could be a physical location, a legal entity (such as a company), or a function that takes place within that legal entity. It can be used to identify a location of something, which could be as specific as a particular shelf in a store.

The GLN is used in electronic messaging between customers and suppliers as well as within companies to identify specific locations. It is an integral part of all sophisticated SCM systems. The implication is clear: IT-related system or data errors or long-term system outages pose risks that could have severe and rippling effects across the enterprise and with suppliers. As a result, technology risks identified in the ERM process could relate directly to the supply chain and need to be considered and addressed.

Other risks include geopolitical risk (country turmoil, terrorism, embargoed countries, import/export laws and regulations), catastrophic risk, and other areas that could impede delivery of supplies or company products.

Finally, there is the defect and excess stage. Risks in this area that may have been previously identified by the ERM process may include reputational risk, if elements of the company's products are impacted by poor-quality supplies; third-party contracting, which could impact how to deal with overages and shortages; and environmental risk, should excess product need environmental controlled disposal.

The Intersection of SCM and ERM

Supply chain executives routinely incorporate the language of risk in their day-to-day activities. Supply chain managers intuitively understand risk across key supply chain activities. But too often ERM practices that could significantly enhance risk identification and mitigation in SCM have not been employed in many supply chain management models.[4]

This is easily remedied by building ERM concepts into SCM activities through:

- Establishing a common risk taxonomy to SCR and vice versa

- Coordinating risk identification, evaluation, and mitigation processes

- Developing ERM mitigation plans and strategies in concert with SCR management activities

- Ensuring that risk-related information is compared and shared between ERM and SRM

Smart Supply Chain Risk Management

Many sophisticated procurement systems are beginning to capture a great deal of information from the supplier community that could be valuable sources of information for risk identification and evaluation. For example, data collected from suppliers that could be useful when considering environmental risk could be:

- Carbon footprint data

- Air and water quality data

- Third-party frameworks data from LEED (Leadership in Energy and Environmental Design) and Cradle to Cradle (a program that promotes a circular economy system in which manufacturers and designers create products with materials that can be used in continuous cycles)

- Data on facilities-related commodities, such as food and janitorial services

Other supplier risk data provided by sophisticated procurement systems could include:

- Sustainability information
- Accounts receivable and other financial information
- Qualification requirements based on company criticality criteria

Each of these elements could be tied back to the ERM process to trigger red flags or other alerts in areas of the company that are indirectly related to the supply chain process. The continuous and transparent flow of information to and from ERM and SCM can only serve to improve the overall management of risk across the enterprise.

ERM in Real-World Examples

Supply chains can be disrupted for many reasons. Therein lies SCR. Such risk, when it materializes, can create significant losses for the company whose supply chain has been disrupted. The following chart illustrates both sides of this equation.

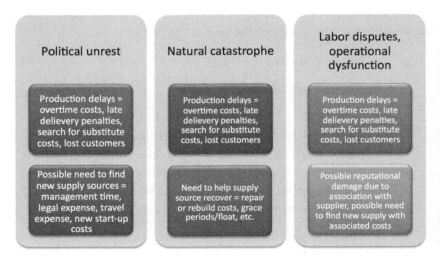

Consider the situation that was created by the Japanese earthquake and tsunami of 2011. On March 11, 2011, Nissan Motor Company and its nearby suppliers experienced a 9.0-magnitude earthquake as it struck off the eastern coast of Japan. The quake was among the five most powerful earthquakes on record. Tsunami waves in excess of forty meters high traveled up to ten kilometers inland, causing a level 7 meltdown at three nuclear reactors at Fukushima Daiichi.[5]

The impact of this multiheaded disaster was devastating: 25,000 people died, went missing, or were injured; 125,000 buildings were damaged; and economic losses were estimated at $200 billion.

A few days after the event, the **New York Times** reporter Steve Lohr reported, "A General Motors truck plant in Louisiana announced on Thursday that it was shutting down temporarily for lack of Japanese-made parts. More made-in-Japan supply chain travails are expected."[6]

The Congressional Research Service had issued a report saying, "The effect of these disasters has been first and foremost borne by Japanese automakers, which closed many of their Japanese assembly plants for several weeks as they assessed their supply chain issues and impact on their Tier 1, 2, and 3 suppliers. Japanese motor vehicle plants in other parts of the world have also been affected, including facilities owned by Toyota, Nissan, Honda, and other manufacturers in the Midwest and South of the United States. Detroit 3 automakers, by contrast, are less affected, although they, too, have taken extraordinary steps to keep production moving, including visiting suppliers in Japan to help them rebuild, locating alternative sources for some parts and chemicals, and shifting plants' summer vacations to accommodate the loss of parts."[7]

However, Nissan seemed to experience much less of an impact than other Japanese and worldwide automakers.[8]

In the weeks following the catastrophic earthquake, 80% of the automotive plants in Japan suspended production. Nissan's production capacity was perceived to have suffered most from the disaster compared to its competitors. Six production facilities and fifty of the firm's critical suppliers suffered severe damage. The result was a loss of production capacity equivalent to approximately 270,000 automobiles.

Despite this devastation, Nissan's recovery was remarkable. During the next six months, Nissan's production in Japan decreased by only 3.8%, compared to an industry-wide decrease of 24.8%. Nissan ended 2011 with an increase in production of 9.3%, compared to a reduction of 9.3% industry wide.

How was Nissan able to successfully navigate a disruption of this magnitude so successfully? According to an MIT/Pricewaterhouse Coopers study:[9]

1. To start, Nissan adhered to the principles of its risk management philosophy. It focused on identifying risks as early as possible, actively analyzing these risks, planning countermeasures, and rapidly implementing them.

2. Nissan's continuous readiness plan included an earthquake emergency response plan, a business continuity plan, and disaster simulation training, and was deployed in its risk management framework and among its suppliers.

3. Local management was empowered to make decisions quickly without needing buy-in from higher-ups.

4. The supply chain model structure was flexible: It was decentralized but had strong central control when needed.

5. Product lines were simplified.

6. Internal and external business functions were well coordinated.

In recent times there has been labor unrest among dock workers in San Diego and Long Beach, which delayed deliveries to manufacturers; labor unrest in China; political unrest in the Mideast, Russia, and Ukraine; and earthquakes and volcanic rumblings in different parts of world. All of these types of events can strain the supply chain, whether what was coming out of these areas was a service (such as computer code writing), parts (such as computer chips), or transportation and logistics.[10]

Through ERM the risk and the mitigation action plans are discovered, documented and enacted. The mitigation actions should serve to reduce the potential impact of supply chain disruption by reducing dependence on certain suppliers, building more inventory, setting reserves for supply chain disruption costs and assorted other techniques. These will serve to reduce the expense and other costly exposures created by supply chain disruption, which are inevitable.

The Value of ERM Relative to Supply Chain Risk

There are a number of key areas where ERM practices should be considered in determining SCR:[11]

- SCRs are enterprise in nature. They can emanate from many different areas of the company. SCRs in one area can easily manifest themselves as risks that affect the entire supply chain and the entire organization.

- Risk from individual areas of the supply chain should be evaluated on a comparable basis. It is important to establish levels of risk using common scales. It is fine if more granular levels are required for an individual area, but for evaluating the SCR for the enterprise, more common levels are required.

- There is a tendency for risk managers to focus only on specific risks within a specific unit to determine the mitigation. Individual risks can quickly affect many areas of the business. By sharing these risk transparently between the supply chain risk management council and the enterprise risk committee, small issues that might have a rippling affect and be magnified across the enterprise can be recognized and dealt with.

- Ensure that SCRM is closely integrated with operations management. The risk function should be imbedded within the day-to-day operational management of the company to be effective. Consistent with the principles of MBO, if the individuals who are responsible for carrying out day-to-day operations are knowledgeable and involved with the identification and management of risk, the enterprise as a whole will be better served.

Chapter 12

The Value of Applying ERM to Information Technology

Information Technology

The state of technology today has become extraordinarily complex, infiltrating every corner of our world. To ensure some level of confidence and consistency, numerous international standards have been developed for all aspects of the technology environment from software to hardware to communication protocols, security and privacy.

Although the each standard is designed for and focused on one specific aspect of technology, they all have one common element of concern – risk management.

The concern for effectively managing risk is pervasive throughout the business community and especially within the technology component of business. This is for a good reason, in many cases our lives may depend on it – literally.

From financial security and stability, to transportation reliability, to communications, medical systems, and personal technologies such as smartphones and home wireless applications dependability, technology is not only embedded in embedded in our everyday lives but also vital to our lives.

Physicians can control pace makers over the Internet. We have instant access to vast amounts of data, some of which would have been inconceivable only a few years ago. And the ability to reach out and contact other individuals world wide have and will continue to have a profound impact on how we live and what we should be concerned about.

Unfortunately threats pervade technology and grow as they become more complex, and those who would do us harm become more sophisticated. A recent news report revealed that the potential even exists for hackers to compromise aircraft onboard control systems.[1]

But beyond the threats of attack, is the need for reliability, compatibility, and consistency, thus the development of regulations and standards.

Although there are variations on which elements of risk each standard addresses, all of the aspects can and should be considered within a well-defined ERM program. As such, the ERM program can and should become the "center of excellence" for risk concerns and considerations for all of the standards.

The value of a well-defined ERM program, then, is clear. It provides a consolidated, centralized, consistent and collaborative means of coordinating and satisfying the multiple risk management requirements of these diverse standards while reaching into and relating the risk within each technology to strategic goals and objectives. Let's explore a few of those standards.

IT Governance ISO/IEC 38500

ISO/IEC 38500 is an international standard for governance of information technology (IT). It is jointly published by the International Organization for Standardization (ISO) and the International Electrotechnical Commission (IEC). The purpose of the standard is to provide an organization with guidelines for governing the use of technology in consideration of legal, regulatory, and ethical responsibilities.[2]

It is designed to be used by all types and sizes of private companies, not-for-profit organizations and governments, providing principles for directors and officers in the acceptable use of IT. The standard ensures that accountability is assigned for use of IT and meeting required information system security requirements including encryption on portable technology devices that store and transmit personal data.

The primary goals of this IT governance standard is to assure that IT provides value to the organization, oversee management's performance and mitigate associated IT related risks. To accomplish this, the framework provides definitions, principles and a model in six key areas described below with their respective consideration of risk:

1. Responsibility. The IT function understands and accepts it responsibilities (and risks) for the supply of and demand for IT resources. The IT function should also have adequate authority to carry out those responsibilities.

2. IT Strategy. Business strategy (and therefore risk) should be aligned with current and future capabilities of its IT function.

3. Acquisitions. A business case for all IT acquisitions should be made including considerations for related business risk.

4. IT Performance. The IT function should support the enterprise as a whole and provide a level of service and quality required to meet business

requirements including management of certain risks such as information security and business continuity.

5. Conformance. The IT function must comply with legislation and regulations, including requirements for information security and privacy.

6. Human Behavior. IT policies and practices should demonstrate respect for human resources in the enterprise, thus contributing to the management of HR risk.

While each of these principles are applied directly to IT, they are also directly related to a number of risk categories discussed in previous chapters of this book. Satisfying enterprise risk management elements related to governance apply directly to the responsibility principle of ISO/IEC 38500:2015. If risk elements of the business strategy are appropriately considered, they should consider and incorporate elements of the IT strategy. Each of these key principles are likely to have been considered across other elements of the enterprise, and if not, should be. It follows then that value of a formal ERM process dovetails if not satisfies each of the key elements of this standard. The enterprise risk management team needs to understand the requirements of this standard just as IT management should understand the organizational ERM process.

Like ERM, IT governance should involve individuals from all levels within the organization from the board to line employees.

A sound IT governance framework can be used to establish a strong link to components of an ERM process which may reach well beyond IT. ERM is a gateway, or perhaps more appropriately labeled, a pathway for IT governance to touch all other aspects of the organization.

This can be done through board-level direction wherein accountability for decisions that impact on the successful achievement of strategic objectives is clearly delegated.

It should not be considered that IT governance has a broader responsibly to govern the organization as a whole. The primary focus of IT governance should be the stewardship of IT resources on behalf of management. However, IT governance can draw from and contribute significantly to the overall management of risk across the enterprise.

In many respects, a sound IT Governance program can find its center in Enterprise Risk Management.

Data Governance

While IT governance addresses the IT function overall, data governance narrows the focus a bit to actual electronic information created, collected, used, managed, maintained, and stored by the IT function. It is important to note, however, that unlike IT Governance and IT Security standards, (which will be discussed next), there are no formal international standards for data governance. At this point, data governance is simply the product of companies and individuals who recognize the need to define the best practices and approaches for sound management of data. This should in no way minimize the importance of data governance. Just as management by objectives (MBO), although having no officially recognized international standard, is recognized and utilized to improve the management of companies, so too, data governance is recognized and utilized to improve the management of data. It is quite possible that international standards may emerge in this area, but as of right now, it is, as ERM is, a sound management discipline.

Data governance ensures that data developed, collected and/or maintained by a company meets precise established standards, that important data assets are formally managed throughout the enterprise, and that data can be relied upon. And it establishes accountability for events that may occur due to data of poor quality.

Elements of governance may include what is already described in a company's data model, business rules or established data definitions or other technical requirements. It should also include assurance that maintained data is reliable, recoverable, protected and secure. While the first set of requirements may relate to efficiency and reliability of processing, these last few relate directly to managing risk.

ERM then can add significant value to the development of data governance elements by ensuring that risk considerations are incorporated in various element of a data governance model.

According to SAS Institute, Inc., there are a number of risk elements that should be considered in a formal Data Governance model.[3] Many of these risks correspond directly to the categories of risk as we have described in **Enterprise Risk Management: Straight to the Point.**[4] They include:

Business and Financial Risk

How will the data management contribute to or put business or financial objectives at-risk? These risk issues may include data quality, reliability, security, continuity/recovery and privacy.

Related ERM Risk Categories may include:

- Financial;
- Industry/Market;
- and IT risks

Reporting

A significant amount of data is subject to reporting requirement of regulatory mandates such as Sarbanes-Oxley, Basel II or industry standards such as PCI-DSS, requiring that data be accurate, auditable, and verifiable.

Related ERM Risk Categories may include:

- Financial;
- HR;
- Legal/Regulatory; and
- Environmental

Business Relationships

This element requires companies to understand and have clear documentation of parties and organizations that may need, require access to or use of data for third party purposes. An example might be access to credit ratings by companies who need this information for their individual business purpose, such as banks, credit card companies, insurance companies, etc. It is also required in consideration of various acts of congress including the US Patriot Act, Bank Secrecy Act, Gramm-Leach-Bliley and others.

Related ERM Risk Categories may include:

- Financial;
- Industry/Market;
- Legal/Regulatory; and
- IT Risk

Protection

Protection of data (security and privacy) seems to be a foregone requirement in today's business world. Yet, we continue to see the result of shortcomings in this area. Part of the reason this risk is so persistent is due to the continual change in technology that may render previous safeguarding measures obsolete. But it may also be the result of lapses in efforts to maintain protection or simply the belief that issues such as this never happen to our company. Regardless of the reason, insufficient protection can have serious consequences to the company and are related to many risk categories. In fact, shortcomings in this area of data governance can be related to all twelve risk categories described in *Enterprise Risk Management: Straight to the Point*[5]

Limitation of Use

This addresses the risk of how the data is used, who is able to use it, what may be shared, what needs secondary authentication and any and all matters related to the who/what/where/and how questions about the data. It is generally described in corporate policy, but also may be determined by contract or general agreement.

Related ERM risk categories may include:

- Industry/Market;
- Legal/Regulatory;
- Contracts and Third party relationships; and
- Human Resources.

In short, each of these elements of data governance relates to one or more of the risk categories of a well-defined ERM Program. The following table is a sample of how these categories can be related and coordinated to ensure seamless integration between ERM and the five key elements of data governance:

	Business and Financial	Reporting	Business Relationships	Protection	Limitation of Use
Financial	X	X		X	
Geopolitical			X	X	
Strategic	X		X	X	X
HR		X	X	X	X
Environmental				X	
IT			X	X	
Legal/Regulatory	X	X	X	X	X
Industry/Market	X			X	X
Catastrophic				X	
Operational				X	
Contractual	X	X	X	X	X
Reputational	X	X	X	X	X

Common themes of both IT Governance and Data Governance center on the need to manage risk. Although the relationships outlined in the table may be unique to each organization, it behooves each organization to develop such a matrix to ensure data governance risk is tied tightly to ERM risk categories. This will enable the organization to gain the greatest value from both initiatives.

COBIT - Control Objectives for Information and Related Technology

COBIT is a framework created by ISACA (Information Security and Control Association) designed to improve the management and governance of information technology.[6] COBIT covers a wide range of areas including Audit and Assurance, Information Security, Regulatory and Compliance, Governance, and of course, Risk Management.

The Risk management element of COBIT attempts to ensure stakeholders have a better understanding of current risk and the impact they will have on the enterprise as a whole. It provides guidance on how to manage IT related risks, how to measure the level of risk, how to establish an appropriate risk culture, guidance on the cost of mitigation against expected loss, and how to integrate IT risk management with enterprise risk management to improve the understanding of risk across internal and external stakeholders. As such, risk management touches each of the other four elements of COBIT.

ISO/IEC 27005:2011 Information security risk management

ISO/IEC 27005 is designed to ensure that an organization carefully considers security as it relates to organizational risks as a whole. It encourages an organization to consider the most significant risk to the organization first in the interest of providing the best security protection in the most cost effective manner.[7]

The standard provides guidelines for and supports the general concepts of ISO/IEC 27001 Information Security Management and all other standards in the ISO 27000 series.

While it seems the importance of security is self evident and well understood, it has often been considered well after-the-fact, or implemented in a knee-jerk fashion that attempts to stem the tide of the security issue de jure. Security practices simply cannot be conducted in this manner.

The standard is well designed to guide an organization to view the risks and implement an appropriate level of security that addresses those risks. Collectively those measures should make up the security program as a whole. And as such, a sound IT security system is built on a foundation of risk management.

The most critical aspect of an IT security management process is to be agile and responsive. And even more than just responsive, anticipatory, in terms of new IT related risks. Perhaps more than any other discipline with the organization, IT Security must be tied tightly to the formal enterprise risk management process. It must know of changes to strategy, marketing direction, laws, regulations and essentially all of the risk categories as described above. It must also be in a position to advise the enterprise risk managers of critical and sensitive changes to technology being employed by the organization or that could be employed to ensure that the business function understands the risks and impacts IT could have on strategy and operations.

In effect, the CISO (Chief Information Security Officer) and the CRO (Chief Risk Officer) should possibly be more tightly coupled than any other two functions within the organization. They have a truly symbiotic relationship providing information to and gathering information from each other.

While the standard does not recommend any specific method of risk management, it is clear that it implies an approach that is very consistent with ISO/IEC 31000 – Risk management. This method includes the following steps:

- Establish the risk management context or objectives;

- Quantitatively or qualitatively assess relevant risks, in consideration of information value, threats, existing controls and vulnerabilities, based on the likelihood and impact (consequence) of incidents or scenarios;

- Mitigate the risks appropriately, using the level of risk to prioritize them;

- Report the status of risk to keep stakeholders informed throughout the process; and

- Monitor and review risks on an ongoing basis, identifying and responding to significant changes as appropriate.

As you will note, this approach is consistent with the approach described in ***Enterprise Risk Management: Straight to the Point***, which is based on ISO/IEC 31000. This of course is not by accident and underscores our view of ISO/IEC being the preeminent standard related to enterprise risk management.

As these two standards (ISO/IEC 31000 and ISO/IEC 27005 are so tightly coupled, it may be the two are used as models for each other on how to approach the management of risk and security within an organization.

In an excellent paper written by Margaret Stoll of the University on Innsbruck, entitled *From Information Security Management to Enterprise Risk Management*, Stoll suggested that "Given the central role of information security management and the common goals with enterprise risk management, organizations need guidance how to extend information security management in order to fulfill enterprise risk management requirements."[8]

We would suggest that the reverse is equally true.

IT security and enterprise risk management, to a large degree, were established to deal with the unknown. Both disciplines have had extensive experience explaining the prospect and potential impact of some event that has yet to occur. Recommended mitigation of the unrealized risk is based, to some degree if not significantly on probabilities of potential scenarios and impact that, if prevented, may not be noticed at all.

Few can articulate the actual value of a security breach being prevented, or value of a reputation being protected by mitigating a given risk.

These two disciplines, being born of similar circumstance and subject to similar skepticism can benefit significantly by traveling a similar path to achieving their goals. So, it is best if they travel that path together.

The Value of ERM Relative to Information Technology

Each of these standards finds some common ground in enterprise risk management. From IT governance (management) to data (information) to IT controls and IT security, each provides much of the same guidance and direction as many of the other standards and guidelines. Would it not be advisable, from a cost and coordination perspective to consider centralizing the risk elements of each of these initiatives within the framework of an Enterprise Risk Management program?

The benefits and the value to the organization would be significant. It would enable the risk requirements of each of these seemingly disparate standards to be directly related to the business strategy as a whole, thus establishing an end-to-end link from the strategy directly to the information that enables it.

The simple graphic below shows the relationship and IT Governance, Data Governance, COBIT and the host of other IT related standards and requirements, such as ITIL, for information and information processing within an organization.

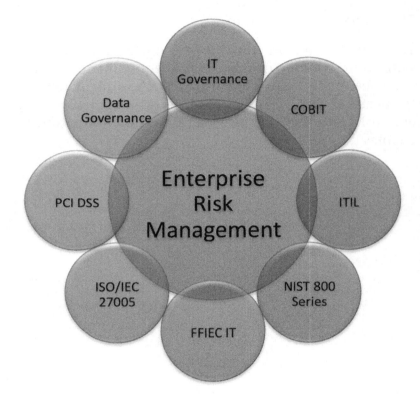

Chapter 13

The Value of Applying ERM to Finding Correlated Risk

Overview of Correlated Risk

Whenever one event can create multiple types of risks and losses for a company or when an association with one entity can create risks and losses for multiple parts and objectives of a company, there is correlated risk.

For example, let us hypothesize that a home décor manufacturer had numerous business relationships with a country in Southeast Asia. This company had: 1) a plant making wall art 2) a distribution center, 3) a call center there for ordering all products wherever they were made and 4) got many of its raw materials for other product lines there. When a natural disaster hit, such as a major tsunami, multiple aspects of this manufacturer's business model got affected. Work at the manufacturing plant near the tsunami impact center was stopped for over one month, the distribution center was damaged and distribution was halted for over one month, the call center was out of communication for several weeks and delivery of raw materials for most product lines were delayed. Unless the company had very robust disaster recovery plans and disaster back-up operations, it faced an existential threat.

This hypothetical correlated risk based on geographic concentration in a lesser developed part of the world may seem somewhat exaggerated to illustrate the point. Yet there may very well be similar situations, in fact. The location or the industry might be different but the premise is reasonable. Global companies do tend to create a nexus of relationships with one or several countries where they have invested in learning local customs and how to interact with the government and people.

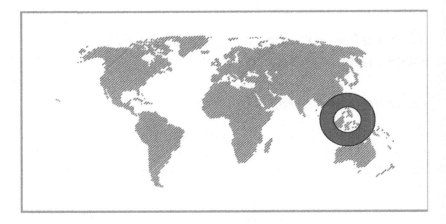

For this hypothetical company, the country where they had so many of their interests could have been hit with civil unrest or pandemic or some other devastating event rather than a natural catastrophe. Correlated risks are not just about geographic concentration.

The value ERM brings to the world of correlated risks is that it: 1) specifically encourages the organization to identify such risks, 2) uses the ERM Risk Committee and other ERM forums to get different parts of the company to communicate risk and to find where correlated risk exists and 3) ensures that these risks are adequately communicated and dealt with.

Consider a food manufacturer that has an ever present risk that the vegetable produce it uses in its food product is tainted in some way. With or without an ERM process, the company has likely been aware of and taken many precautions to ensure that its raw materials are safe to eat so as to eliminate the risk of unsafe food affecting the safety and quality of its products.

However, if by some chance, unsafe vegetable produce does get introduced into the product, this can create a domino effect that goes beyond a product recall.

Product Recall
- First risk involves ensuring that all the product gets quickly and thorough recalled.

Legal Suits
- The next risk involves possible suits from people who may have gotten sick or lost money due to tainted product or the recall.

Reputation Damage
- The next risk involves damage to the reputation of the company that could be temporary or permanent and is influenced by how the recall and public announcements are handled.

Vendor Issues
- The next risk involves the strain on or dissolution of the relaionship with the provider of the raw materials - can they be trusted, is the contract with them breakable w/o penalty, etc., etc.

Revenue Decline
- The next risk involves to what extent will revenue decline as a result of the recall both in terms of the product recalled and spill over distrust by the public of other products offered by the company.

Profit Decline
- The next risk involves to what extent profitability will suffer as a result of declines in revenue and/or extra expense to deal with recall.

ERM goes beyond what might normally be done in an organization to prevent and prepare for a product recall, should it occur. Below are some of the actions an ERM process would have in place to deal with a product recall scenario. Each of these actions creates real value for the organization because each either limits the risk or the impact of the risk.

Better estimates the full cost of the risk of a tainted product	• It is not just the deductible and cost of potentially lost revenue after insurance recovery, what is the total cost and what investment in managing it is warranted?
Ensures all areas of the company are communicating effectively about how they addressing the risk of a tainted product from being sent to market	• What are the staff in Sourcing, Quality Control, Food Prep doing to prevent this risk from materializing?
Beter prepares the organization to deal with all aspects of a recall	• How will operational steps be managed? • How and by whom will public communications be handled? • How will litigation be handled? • What do regulators, investors need to be told?

Counterparty Scenario

One of the more opaque correlated risks for many organizations is having the same counterparty performing different roles in different parts of the organization, often without one part of the organization knowing that another part is also using that counterparty. If something dire happened to that counterparty, or if the relationship gets strained to the point of needing to be severed, the organization has a correlated risk in relation to the areas and capacities involved.

Following are graphic representations of what types of multiple relationships with counterparties might exist.

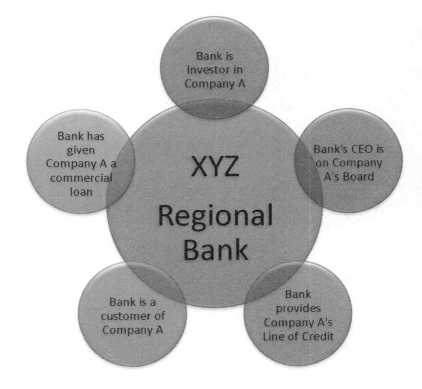

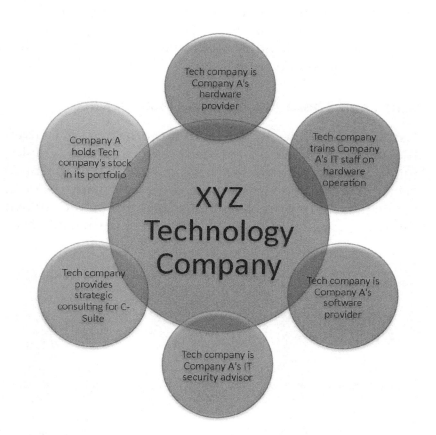

Tech company is Company A's hardware provider

Company A holds Tech company's stock in its portfolio

Tech company trains Company A's IT staff on hardware operation

XYZ Technology Company

Tech company provides strategic consulting for C-Suite

Tech company is Company A's software provider

Tech company is Company A's IT security advisor

ERM, with its formalized process for identifying correlated risk, will help make sure that these counterparty relationships are transparent, documented and that the risks associated with each one are identified and addressed. There is great value in having these relationships understood, for example:

- Opens the potential for leveraging these various relationship streams with more effect;

- Allows for any new, possible relationship element to be evaluated more objectively, in recognition of total weight of the relationship; and

- Creates the ability to determine the potential impact level of the correlated risk so it can be prioritized and decisions made about how much to spend on remediation

And Then There Are Natural Catastrophes

Natural catastrophes are infamous for correlated risks. Given the many permutations of these correlations, a graphic might help describe these. This depiction is not meant to be all inclusive. It does, however, show how many risks can emanate from one event. A similar picture could be drawn for earthquake, tornado and other types of natural disasters.

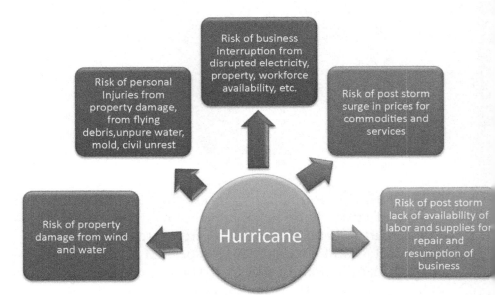

So, how does ERM create value in regard to natural catastrophes? Unlike organizations that rely primarily on their insurance and some back-up facilities for IT, call center and vital operations, organizations using an ERM approach to managing risk have a well integrated, practiced, thorough protocol for dealing with natural catastrophes. The plan would encompass what needs to be done before, during and after a catastrophe. In addition, the plan would take into consideration such things as labor availability, surge in prices for goods coming into area and other contingent issues.

What this means is that the organization will significantly lessen their downtime, and financial and human resource loss and will increase their competitiveness in the marketplace.

ERM Managed Organization

Before	During	After
• Disaster Communication Plan • Business Continuity Plan • Disaster Recovery Plan • Simulation/Table Top Exercises to practice responses and ensure information (phone numbers, e-mails) are up to date • Adequate insurance or self-insurance mechanisms in place • Adequate or appropriate protective arrangements	• Clear accountability for implementing all disaster plans • Allow plans to go into effect	• Thorough enterprise-wide claim documentation • On-going monitoring of claim handling process to ensure timely claims payment • On-going monitoring of Business Continuity and Disaster Recovery Plan implementation • Lessons learned exercise

Globalization Means Interconnectivity

Globalization has created a scenario comparable to correlated risks. It is not so much that one event creates multiple risks but rather that some risk event that occurs in one place in the world – even in a small or remote country – could cross borders quickly into multiple other places in the world. Consider the effect on U.S. financial markets due to Greece's national debt or due to cyber hackers from the country of Georgia targeting European and U.S. companies.

The internet, modern travel, outsourcing, wide supply chains and international financial markets have all contributed to elevating the interconnectivity and, hence, the risk of a risk arising in one corner of the world impacting the rest of the world.

The value of ERM in the face of global risk is, as in the case of all risk, that an ERM managed company is more aware of the potential risk, has more robust plans to address the aftermath of such risk and may even play a role in addressing he risk individually or in consortium with large, multi-national companies which are working on everything from water shortages to cyber crime to pandemics.

The Value of ERM Relative to Correlated Risk

As has been mentioned, the primary benefit of ERM relative to correlated risk is that ERM eliminates a silo perspective on risk in the organization. The lack of an enterprise view of risk is exactly why so many companies have been hit hard by correlated risk that they never realized existed.

Chapter 14

The Value of Applying ERM to Governance

Governance is about how an organization conducts its business in terms of order, transparency, and compliance relative to its own set of stated values. Good governance is when the stated values are ethical and legal. Enron, for example, had a form of governance, but it was not based on ethical principles. Some organizations lack any governance—that is, they have no sense of order.

When a company lacks good governance they open themselves up to the risk of being fined or sued or having their principals imprisoned because they allow themselves to do things that are unethical or illegal. Classic real-world examples involve companies that are indicted because of a Foreign Corrupt Practices Act lapse or flouting other such laws.

Following are some cases of poor governance, many of which exhibit a clear and willful disregard for good governance.

- Enron: Perhaps the most famous of all recent debacles, Enron has become the quintessence of willful disregard of good corporate governance.

Due to the willful and fraudulent manipulation of corporate accounts by the CEO and a few directors and the negligence of its public accounting firm, Enron collapsed, taking its employees, their pensions, and their public accounting firm with it. It became the impetus for sweeping changes and regulatory accounting requirements for all U.S. corporations. In effect, its actions resulted in a cost to all corporations worldwide.[1]

- Tyco International: In 2002 this global company, which makes electronics for safety and detection systems, among other products, was embroiled in a major scandal. Its former CFO, Mark Swartz, and former chairman and CEO, L. Dennis Kozlowski, were accused of making loans to each other without accounting for them and without disclosure to the board of directors and of excessive spending on personal expenditures using company funds. The SEC also investigated the company for possible accounting fraud related to inflating earnings. Ultimately Kozlowski and Swartz served prison time for various offenses involved with how they handled the finances of and reporting for the company. Though the company eventually rebounded after this debacle, this governance failure remains a vivid memory for many of the company's counterparties at that time.[2]

- BCCI: As a result of regulatory concerns and investigations the Luxembourg-registered Bank of Credit and Commerce International was found to be conducting illegal trades on a global scale. Their operations allegedly included money laundering and other illegal activities. In 1991 regulators shut operations in seven countries. Legal actions continued for more than ten years.[3]

- The 2007–2008 global financial crisis: More general in nature, but no less devastating, the global financial crisis of 2007–2008 has been attributed to a severe lack of governance within many of the world's biggest banks, causing the worst global recession we have seen in decades. It may not only have resulted in the collapse of a number of the world's largest financial institutions, such as Lehman Brothers, but also could have potentially led to the bankruptcies of entire nations.

Clearly good governance is sorely needed to stem the tide of failures like these, and sound ERM can add significant value to the process.

Governance as Process

In its simplest form, governance is an aspect of management designed to ensure that an organization operates in a fashion that is consistent with the vision, mission, values, and strategies that have been approved by the board of directors and communicated to external stakeholders. Governance may range from simple guidance and direction to strict controls on actions and operations.

Although the preponderance of governance activities are focused on financial management, good governance spans the full range of organizational activities from operations to human resources. A study by *Business in the Community* found that responsible management of environmental and social issues and their governance create a business ethos and environment that delivers improved financial performance. [4]

The governance process, like ERM, begins with a clear understanding of the organization's full strategy. In many respects, good governance mirrors many of the elements of good enterprise risk management, and, as a result, a sound enterprise risk management program contributes directly and significantly to the governance process as a whole.

Good governance may be applied to all forms of organizations, both for-profit and not-for-profit.

Why Is Governance Important?

In today's business environment, corporate governance has a number of functions that go beyond simple protection of wealth through control and monitoring. Good governance shapes leadership and management actions that occur on a daily basis through a company's life cycle.

A number of overarching factors heighten its importance as well:

- **Globalization:** Markets are globally linked as never before. Geopolitical boundaries no longer exist, and, as a result, problems can spread wider and faster than ever before.

- **Technology:** With the Internet becoming a major part of the infrastructure of most companies, and the explosion of technological advances, including mobile devices, governance shortcomings can manifest themselves virally.

- **Free market:** The view that market forces should be allowed to evolve without constraint has to a large degree enabled major unregulated risk taking. In many cases the view has been that too much governance can hinder the organization's ability to compete in such a rapidly expanding environment.

Effective corporate governance, however, aligned with the context of the firm, can actually create a competitive advantage.[5]

Many academic organizations have conducted formal research on the value of governance. The preponderance of research is that there is a statistically significant and positive relationship between corporate governance measures and firm value, and that governance does matter.[6] Research across a broad spectrum of governance practices suggests the importance of governance to the bottom line.

An academic study conducted in 2003 reviewed approximately 1,500 firms during the 1990s found a statistically significant relationship between firms with sound governance and higher firm value, higher profits, higher sales growth, and lower capital expenditures. Firms with the strongest governance processes earned abnormally high returns of 8.5% per year during the sample period.[7]

A subsequent study showed that buying shares in the 1990s of companies that scored well on various governance indexes and shorting companies that scored poorly would have beaten the market.[8]

In addition, a study by the International Institute for Management Development examined data relating to hundreds of firms listed on the London Stock Exchange (LSE) or traded on Stock Exchange Automated Quotation International (SEAQI) to determine the stock price reaction around listing/trading days. The LSE requires a formal articulation of good governance practice, while SEAQI demands far less scrutiny or sidestepped it entirely.

The research found that companies that had good governance processes experienced an average stock price increase of 3.81% during the twenty days following the day they listed on the LSE, whereas stock returns for firms traded on SEAQI—in other words, firms not necessarily embracing good governance—fell by an average of 0.038% in the same period.[9]

Other specific governance measures associated with an increase in firm value include the presence of institutional shareholders and shareholder rights practices. Research has found that regardless of their ownership structure, shareholder involvement in the governance process has been found to have a positive relationship to firms' performance.

Surely, if the act of governance is this important, then any tool that contributes to good governance, like enterprise risk management, will accordingly be important.

Exactly How Does ERM Play a Role in Governance?

Practicing good corporate governance includes both risk assessment and risk management.

There is, of course, a chicken-and-egg scenario. Many would assert that implementing sound governance measures could reduce a number of risks. Reducing risk is also good governance. Together, governance and risk management lead to a stronger bottom line.[10]

How Does Governance Relate to Risk and Compliance (GRC)?

Governance, risk, and compliance (GRC) is a popular term that has arisen in recent years as the public and regulatory bodies have increased their concern about how large corporations are being managed. It would appear to be a panacea for all corporate ills and as if, if implemented, it would solve all the issues regarding questionable corporate practices. It is important, however, to recognize that GRC is not one single discipline that may be applied like a balm to cure corporate woes. Just as ERM is not governance and compliance is not ERM, GRC is not all three rolled into one common concept or approach.

Governance is essentially a practice that addresses the way a company is managed. It has eight generally accepted or recommended components, which will be described below. These include such things as transparency, following the rule of law, consensus building, inclusiveness, and other practices that ensure stability and smooth operations within the organization.

ERM can contribute significantly to these practices. The steps in the ERM process focus on the management of risks, which is essential to and contributes to the governance process.

Compliance, in a similar fashion, is its own discipline. In today's business environment, ensuring that a business or other regulated organization is complying with the plethora of laws, regulations, and industry standards is a daunting task. This requires a great deal of focus and attention. Satisfying and adhering to compliance directives may, in fact, mitigate some risks. As such, compliance contributes to governance and ERM processes.

Compliance is governed by its own set of process steps or components. According to Compliance 360,[11] there are seven major components of a sound compliance program: establishing policies, procedures, and controls; ensuring there is effective compliance and ethics oversight; exercising due diligence to avoid delegation of authority to unethical individuals; communicating and educating employees on compliance and ethics programs; monitoring and audit compliance and ethics programs for effectiveness; ensuring consistent enforcement and discipline for violations; and responding appropriately to incidents and taking steps to prevent future incidents.

All three disciplines are extremely important to the success of an organization. But while related, all three have very different and important activities. The risk in attempting to consider the three as one all-encompassing discipline is that as in most things, the jack of all trades is the master of none.

The balance of this chapter will explore the various elements and forms of corporate governance and how ERM plays a role in each.

Governance Structures and How ERM Plays a Role

Corporate governance generally refers to the mechanisms, processes, and relations by which corporations are controlled and directed. It may govern the distribution of rights and responsibilities among the board of directors, managers, shareholders, creditors, auditors, regulators, and other stakeholders and includes the rules and procedures for making decisions in corporate affairs. Corporate governance includes the many processes through which strategy and objectives are set and may include monitoring of actions, policies and decisions.

But while corporate governance basically refers to directing an organization, it may extend to areas such as policy development, leadership style, culture, and a full range of directives that shape the corporate personality. One of these elements should be the risk culture that extends across the organization.

Why Implement ERM Across the Organization?

While macro decisions are generally made by executives, stakeholders, and other senior decision makers, most of the decisions that contain elements of risk are made at the micro level.

An article on how to manage everyday decisions in the **Harvard Business Review** [12] tells a story about a company controller becoming concerned about a capital funding request he'd received from one of the company's major divisions: a request for a large chimney. Just a chimney.

The controller paid a visit to the division and discovered that division managers had built a whole plant (minus the chimney) using work orders that did not require corporate approval. The chimney was the only portion of the plant that could not be broken down into small enough chunks to escape corporate scrutiny.

The example applies to management of risk as well. While a corporation may attempt to set an overall tolerance limit for risk, in reality, it is day-to-day management decisions and activities that can have the greatest impact on how risk is truly managed.

So, the first step in ensuring that risk is an integral component of governance is to ensure that the risk issues are identified and understood across the organization and that those mitigation processes are developed by people within the corporation who will be responsible for carrying them out. The daily routine of deciding if a risk is worth taking is made by myriad players within the organization and can collectively have a significant impact on the organization's meeting its goals and objectives. This could easily undermine any mitigation processes developed at higher levels of the organization. As we discussed in chapter 3, the more that individuals who will be responsible for the processes are involved in the development of the process, the more likely that they will be carried out as intended.

Collaboration Enablers

A recent Cognizant white paper describes the importance of the role of collaboration enablers in governance structure. Essentially it says that given the vast amount of fast-paced data that flows in today's world and its unstructured nature, collaboration enablers serve an important role for decision makers and enable a governance model to succeed. Collaborative enablers in the governance model provides a mechanism to share insights and observations in real time.[13]

Other governance modes include the multi-stakeholder governance model. This governance structure brings stakeholders together to participate in dialogue, decision making, and implementation of solutions to common problems and goals. According to Lawrence E. Strickling, U.S. assistant secretary for communications and information and National Telecommunications and Information Administration administrator, "the multi-stakeholder process . . . involves the full involvement of all stakeholders, consensus-based decision-making and operating in an open, transparent and accountable manner."[14]

The establishment of a risk committee dovetails nicely into this model. The risk committee serves as a focal point for the identification, mitigation, and discussion of risk issues across multiple functional areas of the company. The committee also enhances the dissemination of risk information across the enterprise. Further, it contributes to establishing a risk-aware culture within the organization. One way to ensure that communications take place is to establish a risk committee that meets regularly.

The mission of the ERM committee is to:

- Identify, quantify, and prioritize current or emerging risks that might impact the organization's ability to meet its objectives and goals

- Assist risk management in gathering risk information

- Brainstorm risk mitigation actions

- Monitor the effectiveness of mitigation plans

- Stay informed on business conditions to identify potential future risks and advise on plans for addressing these risks as appropriate

- Review the effectiveness of the risk management program overall

Although there is no single template, the committee should include, at minimum:

- Chief financial officer and/or controller
- Head of operations or plant management
- Chief information officer
- Chief marketing officer
- Chief risk officer/risk manager
- Head of strategy and/or head of R&D
- Head of internal audit
- Head of human resources

The committee may be made up of representatives from these functions. The higher the level of personnel on the committee, the more credibility the committee's output is likely to have.

Democratizing ERM

Democratizing ERM serves all these models well. By having a broad base of individuals at all levels in the organization understanding what is at risk and playing a role in the mitigation of that risk, the organization as a whole is well served.

In *Enterprise Risk Management: Straight to the Point*, we introduced a simple concept called democratizing ERM. Once a risk is identified and related to various functional areas within the company, individual ownership of the risks are distributed across the organization. It begins with establishing ownership for the risk, which is typically set at a fairly senior management level, but then the effect of the risk, based on an assessment of the likelihood and impact of the risk, is clarified and shared with everyone within the organization that could play a role in the management of that risk. It is imperative that the risk is clearly understood by lower-level management and employees within the functions with ownership for the risk. Following the example of MBO, mitigation plans are developed with the full participation of those responsible for carrying out identified tasks and a feedback loop is established to ensure that those at the forefront of risk issues can easily report on and receive input from all levels of the management chain.

Democratizing ERM ensures that people throughout the organization are aware of and responsible for managing risks. And over time, democratization will reinforce a culture that embraces ERM.

The most effective means of democratizing ERM is establishing clear owners. Risk ownership can be described in three categories:

1. Strategy owners: These are the individuals charged with seeing through the successful outcome of any given strategic goal or objective that may be at risk.

2. Risk category owners: These are the subject matter experts (for example, an expert on regulatory, environmental, or geopolitical issues) with whom both the strategy owner and the functional risk owner may consult.

3. Functional risk owners: Functional risk owners are charged with understanding risk at the functional level, how that risk relates to the strategy, how it relates to other functional areas, and how it may be changing over time. The functional risk owner is on the front line of executing mitigation processes designed to truly manage risk.

These three sets of owners form the ERM ownership team. Together they are knowledgeable about the risks and focused on how each risk affects the strategy and how it will be mitigated.

Once these teams are established and risks to the strategy are clearly understood, a good governance process should ensure that individuals within each of the ownership teams are made aware of the risk and their individual roles and responsibilities in carrying out mitigation processes.

ERM Governance across the Organization

In a well-defined governance structure, each level of the organization should have clearly defined roles and objectives with respect to managing risk.

The board of directors:

- Obtains a macro view of risk across the enterprise

- Understands and can opine on management's view of risk priorities

- Is provided with:

  o A broad view of measures in place to mitigate risk

  o A foundation for a common dialogue with management on risk

The CEO:

- Obtains a composite view of risks across the organization as a whole

- Is provided a view of and understands the effect risk may play in stated strategies, goals, and objectives and the mitigation processes in place

Functional line managers:

- Obtain understanding of risks under their responsibility

- Obtain understanding of how risk is managed in other areas of the business

- Gain insight into how risk identified across the company affects their function and the mitigation processes in place

Company employees:

- Are educated in the nature of the risks

- Involved in the formulation of plans to mitigate these risks

- Are incented (through performance measurement criteria)

o To recognize and report on impending risk

o To carry out processes designed to mitigate risk

o To provide timely feedback on risk management process that are not working effectively

Democratizing risk will develop a well-defined risk culture that can instill great confidence in the company's continued success for shareholders, customers, and employees, thus satisfying a critical element of corporate governance.

To a large degree, democratizing risk establishes an element of a collaborative form of governance in which participants representing different interests within the company are collectively empowered to make a policy decision or make recommendations to a decision maker who subsequently considers broad consensus recommendations from the involved parties.

Good Governance

There are a number of broadly accepted major characteristics of good governance. It is participatory, consensus oriented, and accountable. Through the formation of a risk committee and risk ownership these goals are well established. Good governance is transparent, responsive, effective, and efficient. By following the principles set forth in **Enterprise Risk Management: Straight to the Point**, which emphasizes a focused approach to risk identification, the process is efficient because it directs the company's attention to the risks that are most significant with respect to strategic goals and objectives. Good governance is responsive to the present and future needs of the organization. By establishing a well-defined monitoring and reporting mechanism for risk that operates continuously, these goals of good governance are also satisfied.

Eight Elements of Good Governance

The eight most well-established and broadly accepted elements of good governance are the rule of law, transparency, responsiveness, consensus orientation, equity and inclusiveness, effectiveness and efficiency, accountability, and participation.

Rule of Law

Good governance requires fair legal frameworks that are enforced by an impartial regulatory body for the full protection of stakeholders.

A best practice in the risk identification process is reviewing potential legal and regulatory risks. This contributes significantly to this first element of good governance.

Transparency

Transparency means that information should be provided in easily understandable forms and media; that it should be freely available and directly accessible to those who will be affected by governance policies and practices, as well as the outcomes resulting from them; and that any decisions made and their enforcement are in compliance with established rules and regulations.

A sound ERM program clearly identifies and documents risks along with related mitigation plans. The risks and plans can be made available to a broad range of individuals, from the board of directors and senior management to operational management and employees. This information may also be prepared for the benefit of shareholders, potential clients who are concerned with how well the company manages risk, or even the public in industries where trust is an essential component of the company's goods or services.

Responsiveness

Good governance requires that organizations and their processes be designed to serve the best interests of stakeholders within a reasonable time frame.

Establishing and measuring the likelihood of risk in terms of time frames, frequency, or intensity allows the company to determine and articulate not only the level of risk, but also the time frames within which the risk can be expected or considered. This may be used to serve the best interests of stakeholders and other individuals or entities, such as large customers.

Consensus Orientation

Good governance requires consultation to understand the different interests of stakeholders in order to reach a broad consensus of what is in the best interests of the entire stakeholder group and how this can be achieved in a sustainable and prudent manner.

As described in chapters 3 and 4, the use of consensus in the determination of risk, measuring the impact, and the benefit of mitigation are integral to the ERM process overall, thus satisfying this basic tenet of good governance.

Equity and Inclusiveness

An organization that provides the opportunity for its stakeholders to maintain, enhance, or generally improve their well-being provides the most compelling message regarding its reason for existence and value to society.

It is clear that one of the major requirements of a sound ERM process is inclusiveness. A strong ERM process ensures that individuals across the full spectrum of the organization and all levels are involved. This will ensure this aspect of good governance is achieved.

Effectiveness and Efficiency

Good governance means that the processes implemented by the organization to produce favorable results meet the needs of its stakeholders, while making the best use of resources—human, technological, financial, natural, and environmental—at its disposal.

The basic purpose of ERM is to ensure that established strategic goals and objectives are met, thus producing favorable results in terms of the organization as a whole, while ensuring the best use of all the aforementioned elements at its disposal.

Accountability

Accountability is a key tenet of good governance. Who is accountable for what should be documented in policy statements. In general, an organization is accountable to those who will be affected by its decisions or actions as well as the applicable rules of law.

A sound ERM process establishes accountability to risk by establishing risk owners and ensuring that risk is managed by specific individuals or groups within the organization.

Participation

Participation by both men and women, either directly or through legitimate representatives, is a key cornerstone of good governance. Participation needs to be informed and organized, including freedom of expression and assiduous concern for the best interests of the organization and society in general.

The cornerstone of any successful ERM implementation is participation. This includes management and staff and all functional aspect of the company. No function is an island when it comes to effective risk management. Clearly ERM lends itself directly to this aspect of good governance.

The Value of ERM Relative to Governance

Cleary good governance adds value to all organizations. It should now be clear that ERM adds value to the governance process. As mathematically stated earlier, if governance adds to organizational value, and ERM adds value to governance, then clearly, ERM adds to organizational value.

Chapter 15

Final Thoughts

What have we learned?

Over the course of this book we have attempted to show how and where true value can be found in ERM.

The chapters in this book covered a wide range of topics in the hope that you would see the vast number of areas within most organizations where ERM can provide value, how to identify the value and how to measure it.

An Emphasis on Strategy

We began with an emphasis on strategy where an ERM process needs to begin. Although it may seem a cumbersome task to consider risk at every stage of strategy development, it will certainly be a more difficult task to alter the strategic direction once it is set, if unconsidered risk surfaces during the execution of that strategy.

ERM is a Discipline

ERM is a discipline that, like every other sound management practice, needs to be embedded in the culture of an organization to be truly effective. It is not a practice than can be delegated to lower levels within organizations to carry out without clear support form the top. It also cannot be dictated from top with the expectation that it will be followed unless all levels have a clear understanding of the importance of managing risk both to the company and to their own well being. If ERM begins with the strategy, it will have strategic value. If not, it will become a perfunctory task with limited value to the company as a whole. It will become a checklist that someone completes, enabling an organization to claim they have an approach for managing risk but not one with significant impact. Once established at the strategic level, ERM needs to be involved with strategic actions and decisions throughout the execution of that strategy.

ERM vs. RM

We also emphasized the difference between the modern or enterprise wide view of risk management that looks at risk holistically, and the classic view of managing risk that focuses primarily on risk mitigation through transferring that risk to a third party – insurance.

Although an absolute necessity, insurance is generally only available for risks that insurers have some actuarial basis upon which they can determine a premium. It is also cost prohibitive to obtain coverage for every risk possibility within the course of operations. And still there are situations even with insurance coverage where claim recoveries are just not enough. The continued operation of the company may rest on more substantive reactions than simply being paid for an accident or a mistake. A sound ERM process may address prevention, mitigation, post-loss responses to better ensure continued operations.

A Management Process

We showed the qualitative value of ERM as a management process similar to MBO or any of the many other management techniques that pervade the business world. Whereas some management techniques, such as six sigma and TQM focus on quality of operations, MBO and ERM focus on the quality of management. This is a bit harder to measure but so important to the success of a company. Qualitative value may seem soft; it is no less of a value than quantitative results.

Qualitative Value vs. Quantitative Value

We contrasted and compared the qualitative value of ERM to its quantitative value and showed how to measure that value in terms that could be used to not only justify the ERM process, but to provide real input to critical decisions, enabling a company to make better decisions based on better information. At a minimum, the company will have a better understanding of the cost of the risk as well as the cost benefit of mitigating the risk through ERM.

We moved from the broad measures of value to more specific aspects of a company's business processes and operations. Beginning with strategy, we showed the value of incorporating risk management into the strategic development process.

ERM Value to Business Processes

We examined and articulated how ERM could add value to the highly risk prone area of mergers and acquisitions. How it could help in determining the pitfalls and problems typical in M&A and how to avoid them. We provided examples of companies which have had M&A risk materialize.

In addition to M&A, we touched on many of the more uncertain aspects of most business, such as new marketing ventures and talent management. Where classic risk management excels in repairing historical errors, ERM excels in minimizing the impact of yet to be experienced risks and the amorphous risk of the unknown. New marketing ventures and the hiring of new talent certainly fit into that category. A company may not be able to eliminate the risk, but by thinking through uncertainties, it will certainly be in a better position to deal with the risk.

One of the more uncertain areas of any company is change management. Despite the fact that the desired change may be understood, few people accept that change easily or can anticipate the unintended consequences it could bring. The value of ERM is that it helps the organization deal with that uncertainty and makes the process of change proceed in a smoother fashion.

Risk in the financial areas of a company may be one where a great deal of attention has been historically paid. Yet, we show how additional value can be obtained through employing ERM techniques to identify financial risk as the business landscape changes and how financial risk can correlate to other aspects of company operations.

We discuss how ERM relates to supply chain management (sourcing), and information technology, two areas that are, to a large degree, governed by well established regulatory and industry based standards and guidelines. We underscore the fact that each of those areas have and continue to focus on managing risk and how a well defined ERM process can assist those areas with that task. We also describe how developing a strong relationship with ERM not only benefits sourcing and IT, but how sourcing and IT benefits ERM as well. In other words, we essentially link risk management from strategy to execution and vise versa.

We also discuss correlated risk and how issues in one area of the company may have a domino effect on other areas. If each individual business function contributes to the collective success of a company, then the risk each individual business function takes on can contribute to its collective failure. Risk can no longer be viewed in silos, but needs to be considered across all aspects of company operations individually and in combination.

Lastly, we learned the importance of ERM to the governance process as a whole. Good governance is becoming increasingly important. We have witnessed some major failures that resulted from a lack of it. ERM adds to the governance process and therefore to the value of the company as a whole.

So, we have shown the value ERM can bring to an organization by discussing it at many levels with the organization. It would have been impossible to discuss how it brings value to every aspect of a company, but our hope is that by discussing the areas we have, it can be applied to all the areas we have not.

Questions to ask

There are many other areas where companies can find true value in ERM. Risk Management magazine cited the results of an E&Y survey in their June 2014 issue. The question raised in the survey was "How Do You Know Your Risk Function Is Creating Value?" [1]. While this survey focused on the risk management function, we believe the same questions posed in the survey can be easily applied to the ERM process within an organization.

Here is what the Chief Risk Officers (CROs) who responded to this survey said in response:

- 23% "Integrated into decision-making"
- 21% Increased Effectiveness"

- 18% "Visibility with the Board"

- 15% "Nature of the Dialogue with Board and Management"

- 15% "Reaction by regulators and rating agencies" [2].

Drawing from this response, in attempting to ascertain value, every company should ask these questions:

Is ERM integrated into decision-making?

As Douglas Hubbard has said, risk and uncertainty are aspects of almost any conceivable decision model one could make, especially for the "big" decisions in life and business.[3] A more informed decision is a better decision. To truly add value, ERM should be an integral part of every decision. While many may say that risk is inherently considered, by focusing on risk as a formal process in decision-making, it will certainly be considered.

Has ERM Increased Effectiveness?

In the case study we discuss in our first book, ***Enterprise Risk Management: Straight to the Point***, we describe the numerous goals and objectives of Curation that always seemed to fall short of desired outcomes. Through the implementation of a formal ERM process, the company was not only able to more effectively achieve expected outcomes, but also able to overcome some significant obstacles, making them more effective as a company. The ERM process is just one tool, but an essential tool in improving the overall effectiveness of management, staff and operations.

Does ERM have clear Visibility with the Board?

In order for the board of directors to be more effective in carrying out their role, they should have a clear understanding both the risk facing the business and the process used to identify and mitigate risk. The primary responsibility of the board is to assure that the risk management process is robust and in line with the overall corporate strategy. They are in no way responsible for day to day management of risk. The board needs to be well informed so they can obtain a sound macro view of the risk across the enterprise, have a better understanding of how risk is being managed and offer guidance and oversight of the process and understand the broad measure in place to mitigate risk.

Does ERM contribute to the Dialogue with Board and Management?

This information will also provide the board and management a common ground for dialog about risk, a significant value to the board's governance responsibilities as a whole. Clarity in this area is important. There is great value in looking for risk from different perspectives. To begin with it is likely that management team who developed the strategy, is also responsible for carrying out the execution. They simply may be too close to the day-to-day details to see a risk or not have a broad enough view to know a risk is emerging.

The board can have an independent view and a diversity of professional and personal experience that will allow them to look at risk from a fresh point of view. The value the board can bring to the ERM process can only be achieved if there is an active and open discussion of risk during board meetings. A common understanding and language about risk will assist in the discussion. It should include a clear understanding of the internal ERM process, its goals and objectives and be compared to the company's strategy and objectives, as agreed to by the board.

A common language or taxonomy includes such definitions as levels for likelihood and impact, as we recommend in Chapter 4 - Quantitative Measurement, of this book. The outcome of a well-defined and established ERM process brings all of this to bear and ensures a meaningful dialog on risk.

Has ERM added to the confidence of stakeholders, customers and employees?

In addition to the value ERM can add to the dialog on risk between the board of directors and management, it can also add value to the dialog on risk between senior management and other levels within the company. To the extent that regulators, rating agencies, investors, customers know and understand what the company is doing to manage risk, they are likely to think more favorably about the company and its prospects. More on this below.

Value for the CEO

The implementation of a sound and form ERM process will provide the CEO with additional value. First he or she will obtain a composite view of risks across the organization as a whole. If properly developed, that is, with unbiased and open communications from all levels, the CEO will see the many facets of risk from different perspective. He or she should see a view of risk from their staff, managers and their employees and come away with a collective view of risk that they would be unable to see on their own. This should provide valuable input to the decision process during planning and execution.

He or she will also be provided a view and understanding of the effect risk may play in stated strategies, goals, and objectives and the mitigation processes in place. In short, a well developed and managed plan for risk should help provide an answer to the question of what keeps the CEO up at night.

The CEO will also obtain a view of how their staff and managers, people responsible for managing the risk, actually view risk. Are they too risk adverse? Are they too risk tolerant? Are those responsible for areas of greatest risk to the business plan indifferent to risk issues, thus putting strategy at risk. Are those responsible to areas of lesser risk too risk adverse thus impeding forward movement.

ERM Value for functional line managers

At a minimum, the functional manager will obtain understanding of risks under their responsibility. It will define what they will be held accountable for and what they need to manage to mitigate the impact of risks within their functional area. They will also obtain an understanding of how risk is managed in other areas of the business as well as gain insight into how risk identified across the company affects their function. They should also see the mitigation processes in place for various risks and will be provided an opportunity to contribute to the plan.

The value of ERM to employees

Line employees are a first line of defense against risk. They are in a position to rapidly see changes that could impact the business – if they are well informed on the nature of those risks. To ensure they are, they should be educated in the nature of the risks; Involved in the formulation of plans to mitigate these risks; and incented (through performance measurement criteria) to recognize and report on impending risk; carry out processes designed to mitigate risk; and provide timely feedback on risk management process that are not working effectively. By being involved in the process and understanding the measure in place, they can be more assured that the company will withstand the impact of an identified risk.

The average employee is just as concerned about their job as management is concerned about the overall achievement of goals. The ERM program can go a long way to providing an assurance that risks will be managed and their livelihood protected, providing a strong foundation for continued operations.

ERM Value to Stakeholders

There are two other groups that will also be interested in how a company manages its risk – major shareholders and customers.

The concern investors or shareholder may have over risk is obvious. Hard earned dollars are invested in a company and the hope of gains well understood. The impact of a significant risk could significantly affect their investments. While risk factors are required to be disclosed in a public company's annual 10K, (Item 1A - Risk Factors) it is limited to material risk as it would be impossible for the company to disclose every last detail of its risk.

Likewise major customers are often quite interested in whether or not a company will be able to weather a significant risk issue. This is especially true if the company is part of the customer's critical supply chain or the customer has invested heavily in the implementation of the company's technology. This will be especially important to customers who have a well-developed ERM process that identifies third party relationship risk of their own.

Again while full disclosure of all risk may not be possible, practical, or a good idea, a recent article in WillisWire [4] describes a number of steps that insurance companies have been taking that can reassure both of these stakeholder groups of how well they are managing their risk. While the article focuses on insurance companies, these approaches to disclosure might be good advice for any company:

A. Publish the Risk Management Policy

Currently there are few regulatory or industry requirements to disclose the ERM policy. It is a document that could be disclosed as a part of the company's Annual Report. At a minimum, a summary of the policy could be disclosed.

B. Describe the Enterprise Risk Management Process

This might include the structure of the risk management team, functional participation of the ERM committee, the international standard being used as a basis for the process and the level of commitment of senior management and involvement of the board of directors.

C. Describe Key Risk Mitigation Practices

This may include a discussion of the management of major risk categories; general methods of mitigation and how the most significant risks are managed.

The Value of Using ERM as a Competitive Advantage

By disclosing any or all of the aforementioned items, your company will be positioning itself as a leader in this area. The positive implications of this can be enormous. The value could be realized in terms of competitive advantage, improved public image, and an indication of sound company management. All of which could serve to satisfy the concerns of the stakeholder community as a whole.

Is ERM embedded within the business planning process?

Once the strategy for a company is established, the organization will need to have a tactical execution or business plan to ensure the strategy is achieved. When these plans are developed, or during the course of the year when plans are updated or changed, risks that have been identified through the ERM process should be considered.

In addition to looking forward at expected risk, a well-developed ERM process will have documented risk issues related to past plans and these issues may be revisited to determine if they will affect newly developed plans.

It is perhaps akin to a view of history. Those who do not recognize mistakes of the past are generally bound to make them again. The same applies to risk. The value of the formalized plan, then, is that these issues may not need to be reinvestigated or developed from scratch. They may need updating, or modifications to reflect current business plans, but when built over time, a sound ERM process will strengthen current as well as future business plans.

Another Way To Look At Value – Examples

We have looked at a number of ways ERM can create value. The Curation case study in *Enterprise Risk Management: Straight to the Point* showed how ERM can even create bottom or top line impact. ERM can, in fact, highlight opportunities that risk presents.

Another example of this comes from the company, Paychex. "Risk managers believe in the merits of an enterprise risk management program. But getting started can sometimes be easier said than done, particularly when resources are already scarce. The ERM initiative of payroll services firm Paychex, Inc., however, was able to gain traction by being more than just a risk management exercise—it was about creating value for the company as well.

As a result, ERM was able to identify and develop revenue opportunities that would eventually be directly responsible for bottom-line growth at the company." [5]

Appendix 1 - ERM Value Tracking - Getting Started

So as to avoid false starts, careful preparation for measuring or assessing the value of ERM is necessary.Here are some basic steps to follow before actually starting to measure benefits.

- Consider what factors are desirable and important to measure or assess

- Determine if there are reliable and meaningful ways to measure or assess these factors

- Vet and get agreement on the measures to be used from key stakeholders
- Remember that qualitative measures and quantitative measures and assessments can both be significant
- Establish a baseline for each factor – what is the current or recently previous level of cost, loss, satisfaction or whatever the factor entails
- Pilot the means of gathering data about the factor's trend line that will provide levels on a going forward basis
- Communicate results of pilot
- Refine measurement process, as necessary
- Implement a routine, periodic measurement process
- Monitor results – what is the trend line

Appendix 2 – ERM Values to Track

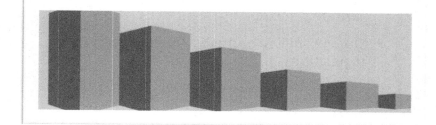

Over the course of ERM's implementation and continuous improvement, the following value indicators could be monitored to track value:

- Fewer strategic surprises
- Fewer operational surprises
- Fewer financial surprises
- Enhanced scoring by rating agencies
- Less volatility in share price
- SEC satisfaction with risk management

- Improved reputation on surveys
- Reduced insurance costs for same coverage categories
- Reduced total cost of risk (TCOR)
- Fewer worker accidents
- Less severe worker accidents
- Less worker lost time due to accidents
- Fewer third party accidents (slip & fall, etc.)
- Fewer property/casualty losses
- Quicker response and recovery time after a loss
- Fewer counterparty issues/losses
- Reduced lawsuits from employees and third parties
- More profitable or predictable mergers and acquisitions

Appendix 3 - ERM Value Inflection Points

ERM is a continuous process that involves all aspects of doing business. However there are certain activities that present more risk or more opportunity to address risk than others. Some of these inflection points are listed below.

- Creating a strategy
- Planning a new marketing venture
- Entering a new geographic market
- Introducing new products
- Initiating a merger or acquisition

- Building a new plant, store, warehouse
- Developing workflows
- Changing IT systems
- Starting a major project
- Creating performance management processes/ incentive programs
- Reviewing, broadening, changing supply chain
- Bringing in new talent
- Transforming culture or business model
- Contracting with third parties
- Establishing financial goals

Appendix 4 - ERM Value Communication

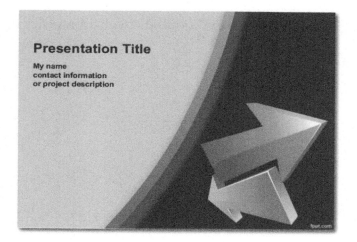

In the corporate world, there is generally a fair amount of skepticism and probing surrounding anything new and about any function's reporting of results. Here are some tips for making the reporting of ERM's value successful.

- Have each function or business unit provide and/ or sign-off on the baseline data and monitoring data used in the report before including the data

- Put some caveats in the report which speak to possible errors, one-off situations, etc.

- Remind all recipients that no measurement system is perfect – in other words, do not claim perfection

- Keep visuals simple and clear – even though there are some recipients who may be impressed with complex graphics, it is easier to explain and maintain simpler ones

- Be sure that those who need to see a preview copy of the report get one

- Check, check and double check all metrics before reporting them

Notes By Chapter

Chapter 1

1. Steven Slezak, "GM's Risk Management Failures Provide Lessons for Other Firms," Global Risk Insights (website), March 26, 2014 (http://globalriskinsights.com/2014/03/gms-risk-management-failures-provide-example-for-other-firms).

Chapter 3

1. Robert E. Hoyt, Dudley L. Moore Jr., and Andre P. Liebenberg, "The Value of Enterprise Risk Management: Evidence from the U.S. Insurance Industry" (report). Schaumburg, IL: Society of Actuaries, 2008.

Chapter 4

1. A number of concepts in chapter 4 draw on ideas from Douglas W. Hubbard, *How to Measure Anything: Finding the Value of Intangibles in Business 3 ed*. (Hoboken, NJ: John Wiley and Sons, 2014). Hubbard's book is an invaluable resource for the measurement of intangibles. As the value of ERM is often an intangible, we highly recommend Hubbard's approach.

2. Ibid, 83

3. Ibid, 9

4. Al Decker and Donna Galer, ***Enterprise Risk Management: Straight to the Point,*** 23–24. Raleigh, NC: ERMSTTP, 2013.

5. Ibid, 27.

6. Ibid, 118–120.

Chapter 5

1. 3M's Form 10-Q, June 30, 2013.

2. Quoted in Michelle Caruso-Cabrera, "3M CEO: Research Is 'Driving This Company,'" CNBC website, June 10, 2013.

3. Associated Press, "As Strayer Education Enrollment Falls, Plans to Cut Jobs and Close 20 Campuses; Shares Slump," October 31, 2013.

Chapter 6

1. James F. Peltz, "Quaker-Snapple: $1.4 Billion Is Down the Drain," ***Los Angeles Times***, March 28, 1997.

2. Matt Krantz, "HP Says Acquired Company Lied about Finances," ***USA Today,*** November 20, 2012.

3. Chinta Bhagat and Bill Huyett. "Modernizing the Board's Role in M&A," ***McKinsey Quarterly***, February 2013.

Chapter 7

1. Company News, ***The New York Times***. June 19,2003

2. "Enbrel reps risk layoff, as Pfizer calls early end to US selling", Medical Marketing & Media (On-line). , April 23, 2012

Chapter 8

1. Alex Hawkes and Graeme Wearden, "Who Are the Worst Rogue Traders in History?" *Guardian*, September 15, 2011.

2. "Hiscox Study Reveals Riskiest States for Employee Lawsuits," Global Newswire, March 31, 2014.

3. "Fiscal Year 2014 Congressional Budget Justification" (report) (http://www.eeoc.gov/eeoc/plan/2014budget.cfm).

4. Steve Crabtree, "Worldwide, 13% of Employees Are Engaged at Work," October 8, 2013 (http://www.gallup.com/poll/165269/worldwide-employees-engaged-work.aspx).

5. "Wage and Hour Claims among Top Threats to U.S. Employers," *Journal of Insurance*, May 21, 2013.

6. Brooke A. Masters and Amy Joyce "Suits on Overtime Hitting Big Firms", *The Washington Post*, February 21, 2006

7. AboutLawsuits.com, "Wage and Hour Lawsuits against Wal-Mart Settled for over $350 Million" December 30, 2008

8. Joseph Harkins and Steven Kaplan, "Maryland Employers Can Be Liable for up to Treble Damages for Misclassification [of] 'Overtime Pay' Claims under State Law" (report), August 18, 2014. Littler Mendelson, PC (http://www.littler.com/files/press/pdf/2014_8_ASAP_MD_Employers_Can_Be_Liable_Treble_Damages_Misclassification_Overtime_Pay_State_Law.pdf).

9. Society for Human Resource Management, "SHRM Workplace Forecast" (report), 2013 (http://www.shrm. org/research/futureworkplace trends/documents/13-0146 workplace_forecast_full_fnl.pdf).

Chapter 9

1. John Kotter, "Leading Change: Why Transformation Efforts Fail," *Harvard Business Review*, March–April 1995.

2. Scott Keller and Carolyn Aiken, "The Inconvenient Truth about Change Management" (report). McKinsey and Company, 2008.

Chapter 10

1. Colin Barr, "Geithner to Rein in Derivatives," Fortune, May 13, 2009 (http://archive.fortune.com/2009/05/13/ news/derivatives.fortune/index.htm).

2. Mirko Zorz, "Risk Management Issues, Challenges, and Tips," Help Net Security (blog post), May 28, 2014 (http:// www.net-security.org/article.php?id=2025).

3. "Aon Risk Maturity Index Insight Report, November 2013," Aon, p. 2 (http://ars-us.aon.com/Global/National/ National Brochures/PDFs/RMI_Insight-Report_Nov_2013_ online.pdf).

Chapter 11

1. "Supply Chain and Risk Management: Making the Right Risk Decisions to Strengthen Operations Performance" (report), Pricewaterhouse Coopers, undated (http://www. pwc.com/en_GX/gx/operations-consulting-services/pdf/ pwc-supply-chain-and-risk-management.pdf).

2. "The 80% Solution: Broadening Supply-Chain Risk Management as Practical Enterprise Risk Management" (blog post), December 22, 2009 (http://www.deandraper.com/blog/bid/33963/The-80-Solution-Broadening-Supply-Chain-Risk-Management-as-Practical-Enterprise-Risk-Management - .VBRRCEumkgp).

3. "The Five Steps of Supply Chain Management" (blog post) (http://www.genco.com/Logistics-Articles/article.php?aid=800607759).

4. Mark Fontaine-Westhart and Greg Hutchins, "Supply Chain Risk Must Rely on ERM for Rescue," Quality Digest, April 7, 2011 (http://www.qualitydigest.com/inside/quality-insider-article/managing-supply-chain-risk-new-millennium.html).

5. Eugene H. Buck and Harold F. Upton, "Effects of Tohoku Tsunami and Fukushima Radiation on the U.S. Marine Environment" (report), August 17, 2002, Congressional Research Service (http://www.fas.org/sgp/crs/misc/R41751.pdf).

6. Steve Lohr, "Stress Test for the Global Supply Chain," *New York Times*, March 19, 2011 (http://www.nytimes.com/2011/03/20/business/20supply.html).

7. Buck and Upton, "Effects of Tohoku Tsunami."

8. Ioannis Kyratzoglou, "Making the Right Risk Decisions to Strengthen Operations Performance," (blog post), System Design and Management, MIT, October 3, 2013 (http://sdm.mit.edu/news/news_articles/kyratzoglou-supply-chain-risk-management/kyratzoglou-supply-chain-risk-management.html).

9. "Supply Chain and Risk Management."

10. An excellent source of information about SCR worldwide is the CIPS Index published by the Chartered Institute of Purchasing and Supply, a UK-based organization.

11. Steve Culp, "Supply Chain Risk a Hidden Liability for Many Companies, " *Forbes*, October 8, 2012 (http://www.forbes.com/sites/steveculp/2012/10/08/supply-chain-risk-a-hidden-liability-for-many-companies).

Chapter 12

1. Kim Zetter, WIRED April 15, 2015 "Hackers Could Commandeer New Planes Through Passenger Wi-Fi" http://www.wired.com/2015/04/hackers-commandeer-new-planes-passenger-wi-fi/

2. ISO/IEC 38500:2015 Information technology -- Governance of IT for the organization – International Standards Organization 2015 http://www.iso.org/iso/catalogue_detail.htm?csnumber=62816

3. SAS Institute Inc. - Data Governance for Master Data Management and Beyond A White Paper by David Loshin http://www.sas.com/resources/whitepaper/wp_51269.pdf

4. Al Decker and Donna Galer, *Enterprise Risk Management: Straight to the Point*, 23–24. Raleigh, NC: ERMSTTP, 2013.

5. Ibid.

6. ISACA http://www.isaca.org/cobit/pages/default.aspx

7. ISO/IEC 27005: 2011 http://www.iso27001security.com/html/27005.html

8. M. Stoll "From Information Security Management

to Enterprise Risk Management", 2015, University of Innsbruck, Technikerstr. 21a, 6020 Innsbruck,Tyrol, Austria

Chapter 14

1. https://en.wikipedia.org/wiki/Enronhttps:// en.wikipedia.org/wi

2. https://en.wikipedia.org/wiki/Tyco

3. SARA FRITZ and JAMES BATES "BCCI Case May Be History's Biggest Bank Fraud Scandal : Finance: Losses from seized institution may reach $15 billion. Some Third World central banks could collapse", LA Times. July 11, 1991

4. "The Value of Corporate Governance: The Positive Return of Responsible Business" (report), Business in the Community website, August 2008 (http://www.bitc.org. uk/system/files/the_value_of_corporate_governance.pdf).

5. Darilyn Kane, "The Real Value of Corporate Governance," *University of Auckland Business Review* 9, no. 1 (2007). (http://www.uabr.auckland.ac.nz/ files/articles/Volume13/v13i1-the-real-value-of-corporate-governance.pdf)

6. Anita Anand, "Firm Value and Corporate Governance: Overview of the Academic Research" (report), February 1, 2013 (http://www.law.utoronto.ca/documents/anand/ TheValueofGovernance.pdf).

7. Paul A. Gompers, Joy L. Ishii, and Andrew Metrick, "Corporate Governance and Equity Prices," *Quarterly Journal of Economics* 118, no. 1 (2003): 107–155.

8. Lucian A. Bebchuk, "Investing in Good Governance," *New York Times*, September 12, 2012.

9. International Institute for Management Development, "The Value of Good Governance" (report), April 2012 (http://www.imd.org/research/challenges/upload/TC030-THE-VALUE-OF-GOOD-GOVERNANCE.pdf).

10. Anand, "Firm Value and Corporate Governance."

11. Compliance 360, "The Seven Elements of an Effective Compliance and Ethics Program" (report), undated (http://www.compliance360.com/downloads/case/Seven_Elements_of_Effective_Compliance_Programs.pdf).

12. Joseph L. Bower and Clark Gilbert, "How Managers' Everyday Decisions Create—or Destroy—Your Company's Strategy," Harvard Business Review, February 2007 (https://hbr.org/2007/02/how-managers-everyday-decisions-create-or-destroy-your-companys-strategy).

13. "Governance Model: Defined" (report), October 2011, Cognizant.

14. Lawrence E. Strickling, "Moving Together beyond Dubai" (blog post), National Telecommunications and Information Administration website, April 2, 2013 (http://ntia.doc.gov/blog/2013/moving-together-beyond-dubai).

Chapter 15

1. Risk Management Monitor - Ernst & Young 2014 insurance CRO survey, "Increasing authority and higher organizational profiles, http://www.riskmanagementmonitor.com/ernst-young-cro-survey-highlights-expanding-authority-top-challenges-for-2014/ April 17, 2014

2. Ibid.

3. Douglas W. Hubbard, *How to Measure Anything: Finding the Value of Intangibles in Business 3 ed.* (Hoboken, NJ: John Wiley and Sons, 2014). 83

4. Guide to ERM: Risk Management Disclosures, blog. willis.com/2014/03/guide-to-erm-risk-management-disclosures/ June 3, 2015

5. Morgan O'Rourke editor in chief of Risk Management and director of publications for the Risk & Insurance Management Society, Inc. (RIMS) | August 29, 2012

NOTES

Made in United States
North Haven, CT
21 December 2021

13499645R00124